Building the Kingdom
in the Classroom

Matthew Pittam

Building the Kingdom in the Classroom

ST PAULS by Westminster Cathedral
Morpeth Terrace, Victoria, London SW1P 1EP
Tel: +44 (0) 207 828 5582, www.stpauls.org.uk

St Pauls Publishing
Moyglare Road, Maynooth, Co. Kildare, Ireland
Tel: +353 (1) 628 5933, www.stpauls.ie

ISBN: 978-1-910365-31-1

A CIP catalogue record for this book is available from the British Library.

The publisher gratefully acknowledges use of excerpts from the New
Revised Standard Version Bible: Catholic Edition, copyright © 1989,
1993 the Division of Christian Education of the National Council of the
Churches of Christ in the United States of America. Used by permission.
All rights reserved.

The publisher gratefully acknowledges use of excerpts from the Catholic
Edition of the Revised Standard Version of the Bible, copyright © 1965,
1966 National Council of the Churches of Christ in the United States of
America. Used by permission. All rights reserved.

The publisher gratefully acknowledges use of excerpts from the English
Standard Version Anglicised (ESVUK) of the Holy Bible, English Standard
Version Copyright © 2001 by Crossway Bibles, a division of Good News
Publishers.

Typeset and Cover Design by MIDDLEDOT
Printed by Melita Press, Malta

ST PAULS is an activity of the priests and brothers of the Society of St Paul who
proclaim the Gospel through the media of social communication.

Contents

To Lucy

Acknowledgements

I would like to thank all those who have supported me in the writing of this book especially, Claire, Lucy and my family. I would also like to thank Sr Anne Therese for her support and Bahram Francis Rafat for all his hard work in the editing processes and for his patience and attention to detail. I am grateful for the kindness of Ann Widdecombe for agreeing to write such kind words in her foreword. Finally, I would like to thank all the young people whom I have worked with for their inspiration and fun.

Note on the text

Scripture excerpts are from the *NRSVCE* unless otherwise indicated. In this work we gratefully acknowledge use of extracts from the following versions of the Holy Bible: *NRSVCE*, *RSVCE* and *ESVUK*.

Foreword
by Ann Widdecombe

The most striking feature of this book is its sense of mission. Catholic education is not about the outward forms of faith but about the development of the inner grace of Jesus Christ. Yet the writer has his feet firmly on the ground and his approach to solving problems is not to seek to undo what is but to find new ways of inspiring his pupils.

An excellent example of this comes about halfway through the book when Fr Pittam is planning for Vocations Day. The pattern had always been that a youth team came into the school to encourage Year 9 students to think about their vocations in life. It would have been easy enough just to continue with this established course, but Fr Pittam observed that the impact was limited because it was just another day at school, so he moved the event to a seminary where the unfamiliar surroundings would have a greater effect.

It is often tempting to think that the duty of a Catholic school is to teach the faith during RE and to supply opportunities for attendance at Mass. As Fr Pittam points out, this approach leads us to overlook the simple fact that God is God in the technology department as much as he is God in the chapel.

Catholic students face exactly the same problems, moral issues and peer pressure that other students face but, as with all priests, the author of this book is bound by confidentiality and one feels that if he were not, he would have some wonderful stories to tell about the modern dilemmas which his pupils face. There are, however, some wonderful vignettes about student life.

Fr Pittam is generously hospitable but his room at the school lacks a sink so the pile of mouldy cups and plates grow until they look like objects in Alexander Fleming's laboratory. As any parent will tell you, asking a teenager to wash up is about as likely to be productive as Canute's beating back the waves, so Father comes up with the idea of asking them to wash up the unlovely collection in the staffroom. Such is the curiosity about this 'Holy of Holies' that the youngsters actually vie to do the job.

Each day has its own reflection, its own saint and its own relevance to the life of the school, and throughout it all shine the enthusiasm and innovation of a truly dedicated chaplain making the book an inspiration to students, teachers and casual readers alike.

Most Catholic schools have a proportion of non-Catholics on their roll and Fr Matthew does not forget that. For example, he adapts the sacrament of reconciliation so that advice and guidance can be made available along with a blessing. This is massively important. I was a non-Catholic in a convent school in the 1960s and we were always made to feel like second-class citizens. Catholic students would pray for the separated brethren that they might join them in the one true fold with us, the said separated brethren, kneeling right there beside them!

As I observed at the beginning, this is a priest with worldly sharp instincts and he also has a huge sense of humour. Thus, he knows that some will come to confession just to grab the opportunity of missing a lesson but for many the experience is something new and healing.

One aspect of this book is particularly striking and that is the role of the school within the much wider community. Fr Pittam visits sick relatives of pupils in hospitals, takes the funerals of family members and generally engages with families.

It would be wrong, however, to think of this chaplain as just an affable friend, for he knows when compromise is not acceptable and is particularly emphatic about the Church's pro-life stance however hard some may find it. One of the joys of the book is the combination of informality and innovation with steely adherence to truth.

The staff and pupils of his school are blessed to have such a Chaplain and so is the Church more generally. Fr Matthew Pittam is a married priest within the Ordinariate. Far be it from me to end this foreword on a controversial note, but if this what married priests are like, then I shall pray for more of them!

Preface

Catholic education in this country emerged in the 19th century with a noble and bold vision to provide for the poor. Over time the development of a network of Catholic schools was hard won. Often schools and educational institutions were opened before the construction of church buildings because the early pioneers saw their importance to a greater vision of re-establishing the Church in this country. For generations schools have shaped and formed many faithful Catholics, although, sadly, over the last few years we seem to have lost some of the missionary charism of the early pioneers. In this book, I aim to reflect upon how schools can continue to grasp this challenge and be part of the life-giving work of Christ.

Through this book it is my hope to provide an insight into the challenges, frustrations, opportunities and joys of working within a Catholic school today. I have deliberately sought to provide personal reflections rather than any academic assessment of school chaplaincy.

I am a priest of the Personal Ordinariate of Our Lady of Walsingham and am married with a daughter, aged ten. Before being received into the Catholic Church I was a minister within the Church of England. Since ordination in 2011, I have been engaged in work in various Catholic schools and also in parish ministry within the Archdiocese of Birmingham.

It is my hope that this book, in diary form, captures the enthusiasm and resilience required when working with young people in a world where they face so many demands, pressures and temptations. Life situations such as family breakdown, bereavement, sexualisation, internet pornography, body image and safeguarding are all explored as I seek to support and enable students to make sense of their experiences.

I have tried to make this a good-news story and there are heart-warming accounts of engagement with the sacraments and when efforts to share the Gospel bear fruit. It is a story of journey of vocation which aims to enthuse others with a vision for holiness, transformation and sense of the sacred. Through this journey I have had to learn from my mistakes and a few such occasions are recorded in the pages of this book.

The central place of scripture and the Church's year has always been important to me and I try to relate my experiences to the readings of the day and the saints.

Schools today are complex places with many demands placed on their time and energies. Teachers now face pressures as never before and with a reduction in the number of practising Catholic teaching staff, chaplaincy is very much at the front line. Its emergence has become essential in maintaining and growing the Catholic identity of our schools. It is my wish that this book gives important insights into the world of chaplaincy, especially for those who are considering a vocation within schools.

As with any form of ministry there are stories and encounters that can never be shared and much of my work will remain between me and the students and staff that I encounter. Within this book names have been changed and certain aspects of reflections have been fictionalised in order to maintain anonymity.

Introduction

The school chaplain as healer

The main role of a school chaplain should be leading young people into a deeper relationship with Jesus. The focus and principal expression of this is always worship and prayer. However, the longer I work with teenagers, the more I view my ministry as one of healing. So much in many young people's lives is broken or fractured and school chaplaincy is uniquely placed to offer a very special ministry. Healing and evangelisation go hand in hand. Often there needs to be healing before we can fully open our hearts to the possibilities of the Gospel. For Jesus healing and spreading the Good News were part of the same commission:

> And he called the twelve together and gave them power and authority over all demons and to cure diseases, and he sent them out to preach the kingdom of God and to heal... And they departed and went through the villages, preaching the gospel and healing everywhere. (Luke 9:1-2. 6, *RSVCE*)

As a priest in a school I have seen that this commission has developed a similar pattern to that in the words of James:

> Is anyone among you suffering? Let him pray. Is any cheerful? Let him sing praise. Is any among you sick? Let him call for the elders of the church, and let them pray over him, anointing him with oil in the

name of the Lord; and the prayer of faith will save
the sick man, and the Lord will raise him up; and if
he has committed sins, he will be forgiven. Therefore
confess your sins to one another, and pray for one
another, that you may be healed. (James 5:13-16)

This passage really summarises all that a chaplain does:
singing praise, praying with those who are broken,
ministering the sacraments for God's anointing, hearing
confessions and seeking reconciliation where there is
division.

Bereavement, family separation, loss, lack of
confidence, physical illness, special needs, general anxiety,
addiction and mental illness will all be realities that a
chaplain will have to encounter to a greater or lesser extent.
Many hours could be spent focusing on each of these
areas and considering the distinctive contribution that
chaplaincy can bring.

In Chapters One to Six you will find the school year as
I recorded it, as a school chaplain, in my diary. In Chapter
Seven I take a more analytic look at a number of the issues
I feel need to be examined and addressed by society at large
and especially for those of us for whom the Gospel of Jesus
Christ is central. In my conclusion I attempt to address
where Catholic secondary schooling currently finds itself
in our current times, especially in a period when there are
fewer vocations to the priesthood and the religious life,
and fewer Massgoers, but in a time where parents, and
many non-Catholic parents, value the standards found in
Catholic schools.

CHAPTER ONE

Autumn Term – New Beginnings

22nd Week in Ordinary Time

Returning – *Monday 1st September*

It is good to be back again. Despite some feelings of anxiety after the long summer holidays I have a strong sense that this is where I am meant to be. The first day in school is important as a day of reflection on the previous year. Today is a training day and the students don't return until tomorrow. The corridors are eerily quiet and lifeless, yet soon they will be bursting into life. There is always a sort of pregnant anticipation in the air as the new academic year dawns.

Training days are important as, in addition to helping a school develop, they give staff the opportunity to grow together as a community. When the students arrive things become hectic and there is little opportunity to merely be with each other. Today was spent meeting new staff and catching up with old friends and colleagues. The main focus in any school during the September training day is last year's exam results. It is always useful to hear this analysis and celebrate the successes of many pupils who achieved beyond what was expected. Most of my work involves supporting and coming alongside students who struggle with life and it is great to know that they did well in their own way. It may seem unnecessary for a chaplain to listen to all these results but it is essential to have a grasp of the whole life of the school in order to be a better support to staff and students.

When all the staff are together, I am amazed at just how large the team actually is. We now number over seventy. Just before lunch, everyone crammed into the little school chapel to celebrate Mass and to ask for God's anointing for the coming year. It always saddens me in a school when staff choose not to attend this central act of worship. In all schools where I have been involved there are staff who connect with the Catholic life and those who choose not to. Engaging already overloaded staff is one of the most challenging aspects of chaplaincy in a Catholic school today.

I have been involved in many schools and most staff that I have come across are supportive of the Catholic life. However, a significant minority are indifferent to the Catholic faith; some are hostile, making it clear that they will only come to Mass when they have to. I don't expect staff to do anything during a Mass which makes them feel uncomfortable but it hurts when some choose not to attend. When teachers and other staff are appointed to work in Catholic schools they agree to support the Catholic ethos, but what does this actually mean to them?

As it turned out Mass was lovely. Despite it being the first day back after the holidays there was an air of celebration and a festive mood prevailed. The sun shone through the windows behind the altar and there was a warm feeling which was reflected in the enthusiastic singing.

The Gospel of the day was the account of Jesus preaching in the synagogue at Nazareth in Luke's Gospel. On this occasion Jesus reads a passage from Isaiah:

> And he came to Nazareth, where he had been brought up; and he went to the synagogue, as his custom was, on the sabbath day. And he stood up to read; and there was given to him the book of the prophet Isaiah. He opened the book and found the place where it was written,
>
>> 'The Spirit of the Lord is upon me,
>>   because he has anointed me to preach good
>>   news to the poor.
>> He has sent me to proclaim release to the
>>   captives and recovering of sight to the blind,
>> to set at liberty those who are oppressed,
>>   to proclaim the acceptable year of the Lord.'
>
> And he closed the book, and gave it back to the attendant, and sat down; and the eyes of all in the synagogue were fixed on him. And he began to say to them, 'Today this scripture has been fulfilled in your hearing.' (Luke 4:16-21)

In the homily I reflected upon how Jesus' words about bringing good news to the poor sets the tone for the vocation of a Catholic school. The Gospel is biased towards the poor and in a Catholic school this bias should be reflected in all that we do. As communities of generosity, schools should challenge injustice, oppression and division. Catholic schools should be places were all human life is valued and given new dignity. This is something unique that we have to offer.

I concluded by saying that in our school we should preach this particular good news through the provision of a liberal education, which works to reduce divisions within our society. However, without proclamation of the death and resurrection of Jesus we are in danger that this becomes no different from the values of secular society. Our Catholic distinctiveness always starts at the Cross.

Back to basics – *Wednesday 3rd September*
(St Gregory the Great, Pope, Doctor)

The volume of traffic on the way to school reminded me that it was business as usual. The place was alive after the summer holidays. All of the new Year 7 students were milling around in tight groups, still trying to find their way around what must seem to them like a big and bewildering place. These new starters appear to get smaller every year and yet their bags seem to get bigger and more unwieldy.

Since I began working as chaplain, Wednesday morning usually starts with Morning Prayer and Exposition of the Blessed Sacrament. Students can come on a voluntary basis before school starts at 9am. Today I decided to abandon this as so many wanted to catch up and chat about their holidays. I wouldn't normally do this but this morning it seemed right as they were keen to talk and not really ready to be silent. They enthusiastically updated me on all that had happened over the summer. One particular student shared with the group that he had been to a Christian festival which he described as an 'awesome' experience. He is now open to introducing some new songs he had learned into our school worship. I am always keen to bring in new music, especially of it is driven by the students themselves, although it always takes a lot of effort and hard work to learn new pieces and introduce them to reluctant teenage singers.

This morning was spent visiting classes of new Year 7 students and introducing myself. I tell them about what I do and all that is available within the life of the chaplaincy.

These are always fun sessions and I manage to share a few jokes. I feel saddened that many don't know about the role and life of a priest, even though many of the students have been in Catholic schools since the age of four.

Lunchtime saw the celebration of a voluntary Mass in the chapel. Several staff were present and a good number of students. We had a full team of servers and musicians. By the time the Gospel was read the chapel was fairly full. I was surprised by the attendance, as it usually takes a few weeks to build things up after the holidays.

Mass today was celebrated for feast of St Gregory the Great. In the Gospel Jesus asked his disciples two questions,

> Now when Jesus came into the district of Caesarea Philippi, he asked his disciples, 'Who do men say that the Son of man is?' And they said, 'Some say John the Baptist, others say Elijah, and others Jeremiah or one of the prophets.' He said to them, 'But who do you say that I am?' Simon Peter replied, 'You are the Christ, the Son of the living God.' And Jesus answered him, 'Blessed are you, Simon Bar-Jona! For flesh and blood has not revealed this to you, but my Father who is in heaven. And I tell you, you are Peter and on this rock I will build my church, and the powers of death shall not prevail against it. I will give you the keys of the kingdom of heaven, and whatever you bind on earth shall be bound in heaven, and whatever you loose on earth shall be loosed in heaven.' Then he strictly charged the disciples to tell no one that he was the Christ. (Matthew 16:13-20)

During a brief homily I considered how the last question was more personal and about belief and discipleship, whereas the first question was more general. The first question can be answered without revealing our own opinion, but the second requires an answer from the heart, which Peter certainly gave in his declaration. I then posed the question to those present: Who do you say Jesus is?

End of the first week – *Friday 5th September*

During Mass this morning we read from Luke's Gospel:

> And they said to him, 'The disciples of John fast often and offer prayers, and so do the disciples of the Pharisees, but yours eat and drink.' And Jesus said to them, 'Can you make wedding guests fast while the bridegroom is with them? The days will come, when the bridegroom is taken away from them, and then they will fast in those days.' He told them a parable also: 'No one tears a piece from a new garment and puts it upon an old garment; if he does, he will tear the new, and the piece from the new will not match the old. And no one puts new wine into old wineskins; if he does, the new wine will burst the skins and it will be spilled, and the skins will be destroyed. But new wine must be put into fresh wineskins. And no one after drinking old wine desires new; for he says, "The old is good."' (Luke 5:33-39)

This gives a great message for those working in Catholic schools. Jesus makes the point that by cutting out a new piece of cloth you ruin both the old and new. There is no use just taking a piece of Jesus teaching and trying to fit it into another programme. His Kingdom-building programme comes as a whole. We can't simply fit Jesus' teaching into our old way of thinking. We have to accept the new thing completely or not at all. Values can often be spoken about in Catholic schools as completely detached from anything else that Jesus says or does. It is our responsibility to present and live by the entire package if we are to be Kingdom-builders.

For many year-groups the main celebration in school each week is the Friday Mass. Every occasion involves a different form group of about thirty students being responsible for reading, presenting the offertory, providing altar servers and leading the bidding prayers. When I first began working in school it was a said celebration, but now we have music thanks to a small and dedicated group of students and a number of volunteers who also come to Mass. We also now have a committed team of altar servers who faithfully turn up each week.

In addition to myself there are usually a few members of staff present including the form tutor, librarian and a member of the senior staff team. Sometimes staff who are rostered to provide support forget, or something else gets in the way during the busy school day. It is always hard when staff members don't attend when they are supposed to, as I cannot properly celebrate Mass if I have to sort things out before the celebration and manage the behaviour during Mass. An extra pair of eyes is always much needed in any school. I fully understand the competing demands that school staff face today. Despite this, Mass should be the main focus in any Catholic community and when people forget to turn up or make other things a priority, it detracts from what should be climax of the school week and our Catholic life.

23rd Week in Ordinary Time

Early mornings – *Monday 8th September*
(Birthday of the Blessed Virgin Mary)

I can happily work late into the night but I am not especially a morning person and so I cannot think why I introduced a Mass at 8am on Monday mornings. This morning we celebrated the Nativity of the Blessed Virgin Mary. A small and dedicated group of students and staff come each week and so I feel obliged to carry on. Afterwards I am always grateful, as this celebration gives a firm foundation to the week, but I take some convincing when leaving home earlier than normal. The congregation usually look tired but the students who attend make a special effort to be present. This Mass is the only one during the week without any musical content and I appreciate the quietness of this simple celebration. Students often drift in during the celebration as buses rarely arrive on time.

A Catholic school can be a daunting prospect for those who have never worked or studied in one before and especially those who are not Catholic. This morning I ran an induction session in the chapel for new Year 12 (Sixth Form) students, who have come from other schools. This year the number of students joining at Year-12 level from other schools is forty-five, which is a significant proportion. None of them are Catholic and most have no framework of faith or religious practice, which gives both an opportunity and a challenge in terms of developing the faith-life of the school.

As a priest it is wonderful to present the Catholic faith to people for the first time, but it is also difficult to know where to begin. Normally I speak to students who have been in Catholic education for most of their lives and it is hard to think of a fresh perspective to present but in this instance there is no background to draw on. I often start by talking about myself and why I became a priest, what a priest does and my own relationship with Jesus. Today I gave a presentation about the nuts and bolts of the faith-life of the school. Maggie, a student in Year 13, talked about her faith and role in school as an extraordinary minister of Holy Communion. She spoke powerfully of her sense of privilege in undertaking this role. Daniel then played some of the music that we use in school and sang a solo. We tried to get the group to have a go at singing, with mixed success. Many of them went to secondary schools where they never had singing of any sort. This is something I take for granted as I have always had links with faith schools where singing in assemblies and worship is part of the school life. I forget that many schools do not offer much in the way of collective worship and rarely sing in any context. Even in a Catholic school this is something that can be challenging but sometimes we don't realise how good things are in comparison.

At the end, it was clear from the questions that this group were interested in talking about faith but also that for most of them a personal faith is an alien concept. One girl asked about the prayers that are used during registration as she did not know them. From the ensuing discussion it became clear that most of the group struggled to say the prayers and were embarrassed by not knowing the words. Prayers that are used during form times usually include the Lord's Prayer (the Our Father), the Hail Mary and other well-known Catholic prayers. Some staff also use the time for intercession and students can lead the prayers. I agreed to produce a prayer card for them to use.

Becher's Brook – *Wednesday 10th September*

During the morning break I wandered around the playground and had a few conversations with groups of students and some of the staff who were on duty. When I returned to the chapel, I caught a group of students, including some of the younger altar servers, leaping over the benches. Being a chaplain involves striking a difficult balance. Maintaining standards in discipline is important but this also has to be tempered by the need to be a trusted mentor and confidant. My role is not that of a friend but I am viewed differently by pupils, who often can see teachers in a more adversarial role. I personally struggle to maintain this balance and either deal with situations too leniently or come across as being too strict.

The chapel needs to be a safe place and for this to happen there has to be a clear expectation of good behaviour and a sense of reverence. Over the last couple of years many improvements to the chapel have been undertaken to try to emphasise the holiness of the place. This has included new flooring and furniture as well as the purchase of plants and two trees. We have created more areas as focuses of prayer to encourage students to pause and reflect. As a school we want students to feel welcome in the chapel but we also need them to respect the place and recognise the trust that we placed in them by making the chapel always available.

I sat the students down and said that I was disappointed with their behaviour. I also talked about how the way that they behaved showed disrespect to Jesus, present in the Blessed Sacrament. They all apologised but I did threaten to lock the chapel if anything like this should happen again. It is hard because these were students who engage with the Catholic life of the school and yet on this particular occasion they behaved in this way. This is part of the challenge of working with teenagers. We grow in holiness and our identity as a new creation in Jesus, but all too often we still bear the marks of our old-creation selves. My challenge is to help students see that they are a new creation but also I need to remember that they are still children and are immature. I am at times concerned that this group is fairly cohesive and their behaviour could put others off coming to chapel events and using the space to pray and reflect. They need to be open to newcomers which is not always an easy thing to achieve with young people. This is something that I will have to deal with over the next few weeks.

Today's Gospel reading at Mass was the Beatitudes from Luke's Gospel:

And he lifted up his eyes on his disciples, and said:

'Blessed are you poor, for yours is the kingdom
of God.
'Blessed are you that hunger now, for you shall
be satisfied.
'Blessed are you that weep now, for you shall laugh.
'Blessed are you when men hate you, and when they
exclude you and revile you, and cast out your name
as evil, on account of the Son of man! Rejoice in that
day, and leap for joy, for behold, your reward is great
in heaven; for so their fathers did to the prophets.
'But woe to you that are rich, for you have received
your consolation.
'Woe to you that are full now, for you shall hunger.
'Woe to you that laugh now, for you shall mourn
and weep.
'Woe to you, when all men speak well of you, for so
their fathers did to the false prophets.' (Luke 6:20-26)

We discussed what it means to be happy when people hate you on account of the Son of Man. Interactive homilies work well in this small lunchtime group and there were some very meaningful comments. One of the students talked about the challenge of being a Catholic when so much of the pressure of life is about conforming to the world's norms. He said that standing out from the crowd, particularly in school and amongst friends, was a massive challenge for him.

Sing a new song to the Lord – *Thursday 11th September*

Proclaiming the value of all human life should be at the heart of the mission of a Catholic school. I was reminded of this in the psalm during Mass:

> For you formed my inward parts, you knitted me together in my mother's womb. (Psalm 139:13, *ESVUK*)

The Church's pro-life teaching should be at the fore of our values in a Catholic school. Non-Catholic staff may struggle with this but we have to be uncompromising in our celebration of the value and dignity of all people and human life. This is one thing that is distinctive within our schools and as chaplains we have an important role in sharing this message. Our dignity does not come from possessions, academic attainment, wealth or status but from our relationship with the God who created us in our mother's wombs. If we start from this point in school, then everyone has intrinsic value and worth. Values of respect take on new poignancy, depth and meaning.

I have completely neglected my prayers today and have not said the Daily Office. I usually say my prayers at home but thought that I would say the Breviary during the time of Exposition of the Blessed Sacrament in the chapel this morning. This is always a mistake as school is so unpredictable and the students who turned up to Exposition wanted to sing and so I could not pray quietly. I need to make my own prayers more of a priority. I regularly have to remind myself that Morning Prayer consists of only one hymn, three psalms, the Benedictus and some prayers. Despite this, at times it seems like wading through a swamp just to get through it all. We should pray because God wants us to enter into his love and not because it makes us feel glowing within or helps in some way. I need to live what I preach.

I spent some time today teaching a Year 7 group some of the new songs ready for the Welcome Mass tomorrow. They were almost too enthusiastic and boisterous. It is one of the lovely things about some of the younger students. Mostly they still have that sense of innocence. It will soon sadly go as the world closes in and they begin to worry about what other people think but it reminds me that we all need to maintain some level of innocence. Jesus himself in Matthew's Gospel tells us, 'Truly, I say to you, unless you turn and become like children, you will never enter the kingdom of heaven'. (Matthew 18:3)

We need to change and become like little children if we are to enter his Kingdom. I pray that in my life I may share some of this innocence that I have experienced today.

Welcome – *Friday 12th September*

The whole morning was involved in setting up and making the final arrangements for the whole school Mass which took place this afternoon. Every year we celebrate this Mass to mark the start of the new term and to welcome those in Year 7 into the school community. This is also the time when we commission students from Year 12 who have trained to be extraordinary ministers of the Eucharist.

We are very fortunate to have staff members who are committed to helping in this mammoth task. Our school caretakers spent the day before covering the floor of the gymnasium to provide protection. Other staff arrange the setting up of the sanctuary and the seating with military precision. It takes some working out to get almost nine hundred students and staff into the hall, each having their own seat. The IT support staff and some willing students set up the sound system and make sure all the musical instruments are working properly. On these occasions something always seems to fail and causes anxiety but everything normally is fully operational by the time Mass is ready to commence.

Later, during the morning, the musicians practised and I collected nine hundred Mass booklets from the admin office, ensuring that each seat had a copy. Members of the Chaplaincy Council dashed backwards and forwards from the chapel bringing all the things that we needed. They are mostly helpful but constantly throw questions at me during a time which is already stressful. I have to try really hard not to be snappy with them and don't always succeed in this aim. Because we use the gym, the items we need to celebrate Mass have to be carried by staff and pupils from the main site: the altar, ambo, vestments, credence table, silverware, books, candles, sacristy supplies, as well as all the other sanctuary furnishings to try and make the gymnasium feel more like a sacred space. This is always hard to achieve and trying to get the pupils to see past the gymnasium to encounter the beauty of the Mass is a real challenge.

24th Week in Ordinary Time

Sorrow and joy – *Monday 15th September*
(Our Lady of Sorrows)

We celebrated the memorial of Our Lady of Sorrows today and Mass was offered for all mothers who have lost a child. At lunchtime we had informal worship in one of the RE classrooms, as we needed to use a screen for the music. We filled the corridor outside with sound and some pupils joined us out of curiosity.

It can seem strange, upon reflection, that we celebrate joy and sorrow together in this way. This is one of the beauties of the Church calendar. We are led through all the emotions of human experience as we walk this ever cycling year with Jesus and His saints. The Catholic faith challenges us to grapple with these difficult issues. In schools there is a temptation to sanitise the faith and pick Mass readings and themes that appear to suit our own needs. However, our faith should not run from sorrow and suffering, as properly understood they can lead us deeper into the heart of God. Without the Church's year we could easily create a purely resurrection faith and ignore that we are also the people of the Cross.

Chaplaincy Council – *Wednesday 17th September*

Today at Mass we were encouraged by St Paul to be ambitious for the higher gifts: 'But earnestly desire the higher gifts. And I will show you a still more excellent way' (1 Corinthians 12:13).

This is an important message for all young people. I shared this passage again during the homily. Often young people only see the imminent and strive after things of this world. The cult of celebrity, the desire for the latest gadget, the need to fit in and conform, all become drivers for many. St Paul calls us to seek something deeper, more enduring and of greater value. Catholic schools should invite students to explore awareness of their God-given gifts and talents and to think how these can be employed as builders of God's Kingdom. Sadly, many of our Catholic schools today don't seem to engender this sense of vocation.

Once every half-term the Chaplaincy Council meet to help plan what will happen in the chapel and at whole school activities. The council is composed of two members from every year group and also a few co-opted representatives of the different groups in chapel, such as the musicians and servers. Today we met for the first time this year. We don't have any members from Year 7 yet, as they are not elected until after Christmas. We had a full agenda. The students are very keen and at times I have to reign in their enthusiasm but today we had a good meeting and thought ahead as far as the carol service at Christmas. The meeting ended in time for the Mass and so we joined those already present in the chapel and offered the celebration for the work of the council and the plans that we had made.

New staff – *Thursday 18th September*

This evening I joined a session led by the RE department on Catholic life, as part of the new staff induction. Each year new staff members meet for the first few Mondays as part of their familiarisation with the school. We have done this session together for the last few years. I tend to talk about chaplaincy, liturgy and my role and the other staff talk about RE, the house system, St Thomas More and the other school saints. Together we give tips about praying with students in form groups and have a question and answer forum. This year's group was mixed with some Catholics, some former staff who have returned to work and those who have never worked in a Catholic school before. The group seemed to be willing and open to support the faith-life of the school and I hope and pray that this will be the case.

Form Mass – *Friday 19th September*

We were reminded in our Gospel reading today about the power of forgiveness (Luke 7:36-50). A sinful woman enters the Pharisee's house where Jesus was eating:

> And behold, a woman of the city, who was a sinner, when she learned that he was sitting at table in the Pharisee's house, brought an alabaster flask of ointment, and standing behind him at his feet, weeping, she began to wet his feet with her tears, and wiped them with the hair of her head, and kissed his feet, and anointed them with the ointment. Now when the Pharisee who had invited him saw it, he said to himself, 'If this man were a prophet, he would have known who and what sort of woman this is who is touching him, for she is a sinner.' (Luke 7:37-39)

Jesus, after some discussion with Simon and those present, forgives the woman,

> 'Therefore I tell you, her sins, which are many, are forgiven, for she loved much; but he who is forgiven little, loves little.' And he said to her, 'Your sins are forgiven.' Then those who were at table with him began to say among themselves, 'Who is this, who even forgives sins?' And he said to the woman, 'Your faith has saved you; go in peace.' (Luke 7:47-50)

All Catholic schools should be communities of reconciliation and forgiveness. Part of human and faith formation is making mistakes and being able to start again with a new direction. At the heart of forgiveness is generosity. Developing a community of generosity, where mistakes can be made and forgiven, is essential if a Catholic school is to thrive. Jesus reminds us in today's Gospel reading that he who is forgiven only a little, loves only a little. We want to send our students out into the world as loving young adults. It is therefore our vocation to forgive and as a priest my role as a school confessor is a central element of this.

Working in school has given me an insight into how daunting Mass can be for those who are not familiar with the liturgy. This is especially the case when new members of staff bring their form groups to the Friday Mass for the first time. I always make a point of visiting the member of staff beforehand to run through things and I call into the form group during the week to help choose any readers, intercessors and servers. There is no expectation for staff to do anything other than bring their class to Mass and be a support. Some staff members like to write their own bidding prayers and get more involved, but others prefer me to take the lead. Today was the first Mass for a new member of staff who was visibly nervous. I try to set people at ease but some things can only be overcome by experience and time. It is good for us as Catholics to realise that there are those who struggle with something which comes so naturally to us. The celebration which gives our lives calm and meaning can be a completely bewildering and angst-ridden experience for others.

25th Week in Ordinary Time

The playground – *Monday 22nd September*

Two verses from the first reading at Mass spoke to me this morning,

> Do not withhold good from those to whom it is due, when it is in your power to do it. Do not say to your neighbour, 'Go, and come again, tomorrow I will give it' – when you have it with you. (Proverbs 3:27-28)

So much of my work is helping students who have fallen out with each other. This often is something fairly trivial but it is often the result of, or is caused by, a lack of generosity and compassion. In helping students talk through their disagreements I am often encouraging them not to withhold good but rather to let goodness reign in their situations. The passage also reminds me of the need for a school chaplain to always be available. There is a temptation at times to send people away or make an appointment at a later date and sometimes this is necessary. However, with young people a few days can seem like a long time.

At break time and after an informal act of worship at lunchtime, I went on to the playground. I like to just roam around chatting to different groups of students and being seen about the place. After the chapel I feel that the playground is the most important focus of my ministry. I met some more of the new Year 7 students, who still view me as a bit of a novelty. Most of them still look so tiny against the older students. It was a good opportunity to speak to many of them although remembering names will have to come a lot later.

Our playground at school is not divided into age groups and yet it astounds me that the students, almost naturally, divide into groups. If I am looking for a particular student, I can almost guarantee which part of the playground they will be on. The students are very much creatures of habit. Spending time like this is always worthwhile, as if I am not careful, I only spend time with those who come to worship in the chapel and events that I run. One of the dangers in school chaplaincy, and a trap I am aware I sometimes fall into, is that we become so involved with students who show an interest that we can neglect our role as chaplain to everyone else.

Sixth Form Welcome Mass – *Wednesday 24th September (Our Lady of Walsingham)*

This afternoon I celebrated a Mass to welcome the new Year 12 students into the Sixth Form. The majority of students were at the Year 11 Leavers' Mass in May and so I made a joke about them not staying away for too long. It was good to see the non-Catholic students who came from other schools taking part and coming up for a blessing. It was also the first time that the new extraordinary ministers of the Eucharist had been seen by their own peer group.

Students played the guitar and led the music with members of the music department and the senior staff did the readings. I am pleased that students are continuing to be involved in chaplaincy and are prepared to stand in front of their year group which is something many will not do. All of the Eucharistic extraordinary ministers are all very involved in their own parishes and so they also are a good witness to the faith. They all took the training and the responsibility of their new roles very seriously.

As often happens, I found that the Gospel set for the day (Luke 9:1-6) spoke beautifully into the occasion:

> And he said to them, 'Take nothing for your journey, no staff, nor bag, nor bread, nor money; and do not have two tunics. And whatever house you enter, stay there, and from there depart. And wherever they do not receive you, when you leave that town shake off the dust from your feet as a testimony against them.' And they departed and went through the villages, preaching the gospel and healing everywhere. (Luke 9:3-6)

Students entering into the Sixth Form are beginning a new journey. Work will get harder, relationships will change and new friendships develop. Temptations will come and new opportunities present themselves. Studying A-levels can be both an exciting and angst-ridden time. In our reading, Jesus tells his disciples to not be burdened by unnecessary things and to remain focused on the task at hand. This message has important implications for these students today.

Our Sixth Form Centre is a completely different building from the main school and was built a couple of years ago. Unfortunately, it was built without a chapel or reflective space. When students enter the Sixth Form many view themselves as leaving the school behind and don't even like to go back into the main buildings. They perceive that they have graduated to the next level and are treated more like adults. This makes encouraging students to come to the chapel, which is in the main building, a challenge. I have tried setting up for Mass in classrooms but this has had limited success. I continue to seek options for celebrating Mass in the Sixth Form. This reminds me of the importance of dedicated space for chaplaincy. Sixth Form staff are very supportive in letting me use space wherever I am able, but I have come to the conclusion that there is no substitute for a chapel or prayer room. Such set-aside spaces have missional importance therefore.

When we celebrate the feast of Our Lady of Walsingham it is impossible not to think of the Holy House of Nazareth, which is central to devotion to Our Lady under this title. Key to the ministry of Our Lady in her family home was the welcome of hospitality. I pray today that new students in our Sixth Form will find such a welcome amongst us.

Preaching – *Friday 26th September*

Following the Friday Mass one of the servers joked that I preached like an American. I think what she meant is that I tend to walk up and down the aisle as I give the homily. I admit that at times I can be fairly animated and find it hard to keep my arms still. I have never really been one to stand behind an ambo or pulpit as I don't like the barrier that I perceive it places between me and everybody else. In school I am also conscious of the need to hold the attention of the students and so I try to speak quickly and alter the tone of my voice. The comments this morning made me wonder whether the style I adopt can also be off-putting to some people.

I have not preached using notes for some time, preferring to appear spontaneous and immediate. However, I do prepare my thoughts beforehand into themes. Often I forget to say something I planned to say and at other times jettison things if I feel attention spans are being stretched too far. When I was training to preach I remember my tutor telling me that a sermon should be like a plane flight with a good take off, safe passage without turbulence and a swift landing. This is something that has always stuck with me. Developing the mental shape of a homily has always been part of my preparation and this hopefully means that I don't ramble into blind alleys too often.

I will think about what the student said. There may be times when I need to tone things down a little and also reflect upon how I can communicate what I want to say to people with different preferences.

26th Week in Ordinary Time

Dressed to impress – *Monday 29th September*
(Ss Michael, Gabriel and Raphael)

Today was the feast of Ss Michael, Gabriel and Raphael. The chapel was more reminiscent of the backstage at a pantomime this morning. I had collected the new servers' albs over the weekend from a parish that had donated them. Before this, the altar servers wore only their school uniforms. The chaplaincy budget is limited and so I find that I am always begging, stealing and borrowing items from local parishes and convents. I have become skilled at salvaging all kinds of things for use in the chapel. For months the Chaplaincy Council and the servers have been nagging me to buy some proper cassocks or albs for them to wear. Now that they had arrived, the enthusiastic servers were diving into the pile to try to get one that fitted. Initially they were not sure of the results until Jacob pointed out that they looked like the robes from the *Assassins Creed* video game. They looked very smart and it is certainly an improvement from serving in school uniforms. Before I had a chance to call them back, a couple of the servers had run out of the chapel in their new albs to show them off. I can't imagine what the other staff and students must have thought when seeing two small figures robed in white walking through the corridors.

The altar servers are a faithful group who both delight and frustrate me. This is the first year that we have had servers drawn from every year group in the school and there are about twenty students who regularly serve in the chapel and at whole school events. For the last couple of years, I have not had a Mass where there has not been a server and often I have to turn students away from the sacristy because I cannot invent any more jobs for them to do.

Often I have to deal with minor conflicts and squabbles within the serving team because they fall out over job allocation, what to wear and who is in charge. I can normally restore order but it is not a good way to prepare for Mass. Keeping a silent time of preparation is always a struggle. Yet when they serve, they do so with such dignity and reverence. I was recently talking to a server in Year 9 about his serving role. It was clear that he was developing a great love for the liturgy and when he serves he has such good liturgical sense. Many of the servers don't serve outside of school and few go to Mass in a local parish. Many of my fellow clergy would have views about non-practising servers, but I am happy to have them involved and always view my role as sowing seeds that will hopefully bear fruit at some point in their lives. I know that this is not ideal and do wrestle with this issue. Students who serve in parishes are also reluctant to do so in school.

Sometimes the altar servers feel anxious about serving in front of their fellow students and occasionally they will face peer pressure and name-calling. This is always dealt with by staff when they discover it has happened but it still means that servers can be nervous before larger events. Despite this, no server has left and they continue to be a loyal and faithful band.

Many of those that come to chapel have become familiar with the prayer to St Michael which they use during the Rosary Club. As it was St Michael's feast day, at the end of Mass I asked one student to recite the prayer from memory. He did so splendidly:

> Holy Michael, the Archangel, defend us in battle. Be our safeguard against the wickedness and snares of the devil. May God rebuke him, we humbly pray; and do you, O Prince of the heavenly host, by the power of God cast into hell Satan and all the evil spirits who wander through the world seeking the ruin of souls. Amen.[1]

---

1. The 'Leonine Prayers' originated in 1884, when Pope Leo XIII ordered certain prayers to be said after Low Mass, in defence of the independence of the Holy See. The prayer to St Michael that we used today was added to the Leonine Prayers in 1886. It is no longer prescribed for use at the end of Mass in the Ordinary Form but is still used as a prayer for spiritual protection.

Blessed are the meek – *Wednesday 1st October*
(St Thérèse of Lisieux)

October is the month of the Holy Rosary and today we said the rosary during Exposition of the Blessed Sacrament. I very rarely use the rosary in school, although one of the RE teachers runs the very popular Rosary Club every Thursday lunchtime. Today I was delighted to see how well the students knew the rosary. One student started leading the group and then got others to take charge of each decade. They knew all the mysteries and additional prayers and the care that they took in saying the prayers was amazing. My presence wasn't really necessary at all. I was also surprised that most students had brought their own rosaries. These ranged from the tasteful to full fluorescent plastic.

During the morning I met with a group of students who are struggling to make friends and have low self-esteem. I regularly run all kinds of groups and find group work to be one of the most effective ways of engaging students. It also helps to develop confidence, relationships and often friendship. Today I concluded with a reflection and meditation based on the story of the Feeding of the Five Thousand and a song that we sing in school, which speaks of us as being the only hope on earth as builders of the Kingdom of God. I read the passage from Matthew's Gospel:

> Now when Jesus heard this, he withdrew from there in a boat to a lonely place apart. But when the crowds heard it, they followed him on foot from the towns. As he went ashore he saw a great throng; and he had compassion on them, and healed their sick. When it was evening, the disciples came to him and said, 'This is a lonely place, and the day is now over; send the crowds away to go into the villages and buy food for themselves.' Jesus said, 'They need not go away; you

give them something to eat.' They said to him, 'We have only five loaves here and two fish.' And he said, 'Bring them here to me.' Then he ordered the crowds to sit down on the grass; and taking the five loaves and the two fish he looked up to heaven, and blessed, and broke and gave the loaves to the disciples, and the disciples gave them to the crowds. And they all ate and were satisfied. And they took up twelve baskets full of the broken pieces left over. And those who ate were about five thousand men, besides women and children. (Matthew 14:13-21)

I spoke of how the story starts with something insignificant and small but Jesus uses this to become a gift to others which is transformative. The small boy and his tiny loaves feed all those present. The weakest therefore becomes the one who provides for all and saves the day. Those students in this group may feel insignificant and vulnerable, but God uses the small things of this world and gives them dignity and purpose.

In Mark's Gospel (Mark 9:13) Jesus tells us that when we welcome little children, we welcome him. In schools we honour Jesus, present in our students, when we give our attention to the unpopular, the overlooked and those who struggle to fit in. This very much follows Jesus' pattern of using marginal people from obscure places and seeking transformation in their lives.

Meeting the leadership – *Friday 3rd October*

At half past nine I had an appointment with the Sixth Form senior-student team. As soon as Mass was over I dashed to the meeting. Every so often I arrange to meet with this team to discuss chaplaincy issues and plan things for the forthcoming term. The senior student team are composed of head boy and head girl and their deputies. They are elected by the student body and staff and are therefore good representatives of the wider community. Their role is to represent the students to the senior staff team and to plan and run events. This is the first time that I have met with this particular team since they were elected. We discussed a few possibilities and put some provisional dates in the diary for future activities and a further meeting. They are a committed group but have many preoccupations of which faith is only one small aspect. By the time students reach Year 13 they understandably become so fixated upon exams, university and their work that all other activities tend to take second place.

Chaplaincy with Sixth-Form-age students is always challenging and most of my work involves just being present. I ensure that I am in the study centre for at least two hours each week, walk around at break times, pop into the art and technology rooms and also take part in the enrichment programme. I feel that this physical presence is the best that I can offer at this time

I often wonder what an ideal Catholic Sixth Form college should be like. I do feel that many Catholic Sixth Form colleges are light in terms of the faith and a lower proportion of Catholic students and staff members can contribute to the way in which the Catholic faith is lived out and promoted.

27th Week in Ordinary Time

Social network – *Monday 6th October*

A student met me this morning with some printouts from a social network site in which various photographs of staff had been posted with sexually explicit comments. There was a photo of me and what really was just a silly comment.

I reported this to the deputy head teacher who deals with safeguarding and online issues.

The students involved have been identified but it has really upset me and makes me feel vulnerable. With all the things that have gone on in the Catholic Church over the last few years, priests do feel vulnerable and I am oversensitive of anything like this. I am always aware that my work with young people does leave me a little exposed to this sort of thing and very careful about the ways that I interact with the students in the school. I am glad that the students involved were not individuals that I work with regularly as that would have really hurt far more. For me this gives such an insight into the world within which our students exist and the issues that they face in terms of social media.

This incident has been dealt with well by the school and due procedures have been followed but for the rest of the day I have had a heavy heart. Social media causes so many issues when working with young people. We hear a great deal about cyberbullying but to have it happen to me has really left me feeling wounded. It is just a sick joke but those involved don't understand the hurt and possible damage to a priest's reputation and standing that such things can cause.

I spoke to the representative from the Archdiocese of Birmingham who was reassuring. I have even questioned the wisdom of being a chaplain in school today.

I found some reassurance and comfort in some passages from today's first reading at Mass,

> I am astonished that you are so quickly deserting him who called you in the grace of Christ and turning to a different gospel – not that there is another gospel, but there are some who trouble you and want to pervert the gospel of Christ. But even if we, or an

angel from heaven, should preach to you a gospel contrary to that which we preached to you, let him be accursed. As we have said before, so now I say again, If any one is preaching to you a gospel contrary to that which you received, let him be accursed. Am I now seeking the favour of men, or of God? Or am I trying to please men? If I were still pleasing men, I should not be a servant of Christ. (Galatians 1:6-12)

St Paul makes it clear that preaching the Gospel involves sacrifices and will not always win us favour with the world. To be a servant of Christ sometimes involves standing apart from the world and taking the blows that it has to offer.

Open Evening – *Thursday 9th October*

Tonight was Open Evening when prospective students and their parents have an opportunity to look around the school. Each department puts on displays and staff are available to answer questions. The Chaplaincy Council had planned to open the chapel and have different areas displaying the various aspects of the life of the chapel. These included altar serving, music, the Rosary Club and worship. Eleven students had volunteered to staff these areas and talk to any of those who visited. The students in the music corner played a few requests and the Rosary Club representatives gave away some prayer cards which they had made. The chapel is so small and it was a little tight tonight with all that they had planned. It was a good evening and it gave me the opportunity to talk to some parents that I knew. A few of the visitors even went to school with me almost twenty years ago!

It is important to have the chapel open on these evenings as it is a reminder of the central place the Catholic faith has in the school.

Teaching the Mass – *Friday 10th October*

There are many who seek to undermine Catholic and indeed all faith-based education. Secular campaigns against church schools are nothing new but seem to be growing in confidence and venom at this time. For Catholic education to continue to flourish and bless others we need to stand firm together in the defence of our mission. I was reminded of this through a few passages in today's Gospel reading:

> But some of them said, 'He casts out demons by Be-elzebul, the prince of demons'; while others, to test him, sought from him a sign from heaven. But he, knowing their thoughts, said to them, 'Every kingdom divided against itself is laid waste, and house falls upon house. And if Satan also is divided against himself, how will his kingdom stand?' (Luke 11:15-18)

Whilst Jesus is talking about the devil, what he says can be applied to us. If we are divided and not united, then our house could fall. If people are not one hundred per cent behind a vision for Catholic education, then we lay ourselves open to those who seek to undo our work. This also involves recognising and acting when parts of the household are broken or need replacing and renewal. So much is changing in the world of education and outside pressures, such as the drive to become academies, can rock our foundations if we are not built together strongly.

Pupils in Year 7 always have a module taught on the Mass as part of the RE curriculum. A recent development has been my involvement in celebrating teaching masses. This involves celebrating Mass for a whole class and stopping at appropriate points to reflect upon what has just happened or thinking about what comes next. We focus on the Gathering, the Readings, the Homily, the

Consecration, receiving Communion, the Blessing and Dismissal.

We also talk at the beginning about preparation, why we use vestments, what the different liturgical objects are for, and prayers they can use to prepare spiritually for the liturgy themselves. I always find that following these sessions one or two pupils start coming to Mass on a voluntary basis and so I am keen that this innovation continues. Although this Mass stops and starts it retains a sense of dignity and hopefully leaves the students with a better concept of the meaning of the Mass. In their RE lessons they have already completed a workbook on this subject and so when they come to these occasions they are usually well prepared.

What is Faith? – *Saturday 11th October*

Today, whilst out shopping, I met a former student who is now at university. She told me all that she was doing and obviously loved university life. I remember at school that she had many issues with the Catholic faith and at one point declared that she was an atheist. I was delighted to learn that she had joined the Catholic Society (CathSoc) at the university and was now very animated about her faith.

In my experience many Sixth Form students go through a stage where they question or doubt their faith. I see this as part of a natural process of development. For many years most of the students have been in Catholic education and in Sixth Form they experience more freedom to express themselves. They are also at that stage in life when they are developing their own identities as young adults. Questioning previously held and inherited truths is not something that I am personally worried about and I am sure that many will have a change of heart at some point in their lives. The majority have also have not come from practising Catholic families and so may have only had a very limited experience of the faith in a lived way. Sadly, the education system and the sacraments of initiation (baptism, First Holy Communion, confirmation) may be the only foundation that they have had. Many were lapsed before the journey started.

This was never my own experience as I came to faith and was baptised when I was sixteen. As a teenager I grew in awareness of the love of God. My family were not particularly religious and although I was sent to Sunday school we did not have any religious practice. I started going to my local church and slowly got involved and for me this seemed completely normal. Sadly, most people's experience is the opposite.

28th Week in Ordinary Time

Collective worship – *Monday 13th October*

Today I led an assembly for Year 7 students. I used the time to teach them some new music. The chapel musicians have been learning some new pieces for a while and so it was good for them to hear the songs being sung in this way. I am always reluctant to use assembly time for singing practices but there is no other forum to get a whole year group together to practise the songs and Mass settings that we use in school. I always feel guilty hijacking assemblies for other purposes as the main focus should be worship.

I have connections with many schools and have experienced and witnessed assemblies in many different contexts over the years. In one of the schools where I am a governor we use an assessed assembly as part of the recruitment process for staff, which allows us to see how they offer worship in this context and how they relate themes and the Church seasons to students' lives and experiences.

Many assemblies are far from the vision of collective worship that they should be. Often so much has to be done in an assembly that the central aspect of worship is squeezed out. This is the time in the week when notices are given out, disciplinary issues are discussed, volunteers are selected for various activities and outside speakers are invited to talk. Part of a chaplain's role is to be a critical friend when it comes to worship. We need to gently challenge our schools about collective worship and also be a resource to staff who are unsure and need some help.

On one occasion, I was observing a secondary school assembly where a member of staff gave a beautiful and worship-filled assembly which had a great deal of student involvement. I remember being greatly impressed by the enthusiasm of the teacher and the time that he must have devoted in terms of preparation. This was completely undone when, at the end of the assembly, the head of year started telling everyone off for things that had happened during the week. I could feel all of the good will and positivity that had been built up draining away as she spoke to them. I perceive that part of the problem is that staff feel uncomfortable or unequipped for leading worship. Training days have full programmes but making space for some faith and spiritual development is important and collective worship should feature as part of a wider programme which is driven by chaplaincy.

It also raises the question about whether staff members who don't believe in God, or who don't have an active faith, can really lead others in worship. There is a major difference between collective worship and common worship, but in many Catholic schools I feel the standard should be much higher. We wouldn't accept an atheist or agnostic leading worship in our parish churches so why would be consider it acceptable in our Catholic schools? I often reflect that there should to be a distinction between an administrative assembly and a worship assembly. This needs to be grasped as for many students from non-practising families the assembly is the only form of worship that they experience all week.

Growing community – *Wednesday 15th October (St Teresa of Avila)*

As I read the Gospel at Mass today I received it as a personal reminder not to try to work under my own strength and effort. This is something that I am guilty of. When I neglect my prayers or rush my devotional life I recognise that things start to go wrong and I am no longer rooted as I should be. I therefore need to take to heart Jesus' words in the Gospel today (John 15:1-8):

> I am the true vine, and my Father is the vinedresser. Every branch of mine that bears no fruit, he takes away, and every branch that does bear fruit he prunes, that it may bear more fruit. You are already made clean by the word which I have spoken to you. Abide in me, and I in you. As the branch cannot bear fruit by itself, unless it abides in the vine, neither can you, unless you abide in me. I am the vine, you are the branches. He who abides in me, and I in him, he it is that bears much fruit, for apart from me you can do nothing. (John 15:1-6)

One of the main challenges of the lunchtime masses is getting the students to settle down before Mass begins. Time is tight and I like Mass to be over in time to allow pupils to get to the canteen or to the chaplaincy room to have their lunch. I am very clear in school about the Church's teaching on fasting before Mass and feel strongly that it is not our decision to lower the standards that the Church sets.

A number of students come into the chapel with such pent-up energy, having been in lessons all morning. I have stopped the altar servers robing on Wednesdays as it is just one more complication in a situation which is already hectic. Today I had to keep asking students to sit down and be quiet before the beginning of Mass. The musicians couldn't hear their instruments for tuning at one point. Often I am the only member of staff at the beginning of Mass. I want to make the chapel an accessible place, but for all to feel safe and welcome there needs to be clearer and stronger expectations and boundaries.

Once everyone settled down, the celebration was dignified and full of joy. There is often a real contrast with the atmosphere before the start of Mass, and the students' conduct as soon as the bell rings for Mass to commence. Throughout the liturgy there was a feeling of spiritual unity and friendship and most students demonstrate a maturity that they don't always show in other aspects of their school life.

This is the same with Exposition of the Blessed Sacrament. As soon as Jesus is placed upon the altar there is a silence, dignity and reverence. I often think that one way to improve behaviour in the chapel is to have Adoration before each Mass.

Prayer board – *Friday 17th October*
(St Ignatius of Antioch)

After Mass today, one of the altar servers drew my attention to a prayer on the chapel prayer board which gave a little too much detail of a personal situation. I always discourage students from putting too much information onto the board due to issues of confidentiality and gossip amongst the young people. I removed the prayer request and later saw the person who wrote it.

The prayer board has been in the chapel for many years and is a place where students can write their prayers. Added to this is a prayer tree, which I made a few years ago, where students can hang their prayers from the branches. One of my jobs is to regularly check the tree and board to ensure that any inappropriate prayers or comments are removed. Thankfully, most prayer requests that are posted are appropriate and I do not have to remove many. Contained on the board are prayers for the sick, the dying, exam results, staff members, as well as situations in the world. If a prayer is trivial or a posting is inappropriate, it detracts from the really meaningful and heartfelt prayers that are on the board. I also ask that prayers for specific students in school do not carry their names so that they can remain anonymous.

The prayer board and tree are really popular and I seem to always be cutting up new prayer slips as they get used up so quickly. Some prayers are really moving and give a real insight into the situations within which some students find themselves. When students and staff stop me and ask for prayers I invite them to also visit the prayer board. It is an important ministry but needs to be managed properly in order to have the maximum impact and benefit.

29th Week in Ordinary Time

All things to all people – *Monday 20th October*

I am becoming increasingly aware that I am not very good at being a chaplain to the whole school. I focus most of my effort on the students and neglect the teachers and support staff. One of the benefits of the early Monday Mass and being present in school from 7.15am is that I have managed to get to know some of the cleaning staff well. The cleaners are so important to the well-being of any school community and yet they are often overlooked. The story of Mary and Martha (Luke 10:38-42) comes to mind when I think about this team of people. Today, I had a chat with some of the team about their families. Many of the cleaners have worked in the school for years and they are very committed and loyal. They carry on discretely in their work.

Today's Gospel was the Parable of the Rich Fool and one part of the passage stood out for me today,

> And he told them a parable, saying, 'The land of a rich man brought forth plentifully; and he thought to himself, "What shall I do, for I have nowhere to store my crops?" And he said, "I will do this: I will pull down my barns, and build larger ones; and there I will store all my grain and my goods. And I will say to my soul, Soul, you have ample goods laid up for many years; take your ease, eat, drink, be merry." But God said to him, "Fool! This night your soul is required of you; and the things you have prepared, whose will they be?" So is he who lays up treasure for himself, and is not rich toward God.' (Luke 12:16-21)

As school chaplains we have a great treasure to share. If we restrict that treasure to one aspect of the school community, then we are not sharing this treasure as we should. When school chaplain jobs are advertised I often look at the job description and person specification to see what schools are looking for, so that I can keep abreast of developments. Often the requirement to be chaplain to the whole school is neglected in these documents. School chaplaincy, whether ordained or lay, is far more than just youth work and some of the most meaningful ministry that I have had has been in supporting staff in their difficult role. Students come and go but staff will normally be with you a lot longer and so it is here that the opportunity for meaningful pastoral care can present itself.

Performance review – *Wednesday 22nd October*

How does a chaplain measure their successes? This is an impossible question to answer. Much of what a chaplain does is not quantifiable and our work largely remains unknown. Fruits of what we do may only emerge years later. Today I received the paperwork for my performance review. Every year all staff members have to complete this review with their line manager. This involves reflecting about what has happened during the last year and setting targets for the forthcoming year. I can easily set targets but so much of my work is in building individual relationships and supporting students and staff to develop their spiritual lives. This year I set three targets: developing music, increasing student involvement in worship and deepening my work in the Sixth Form. These are achievable and can be measured to a certain extent. However, if I were to think of successes from last year they would include encouraging a vulnerable child to read at Mass for the first time, building a trusting relationship with a student who had been abused, and supporting students to make a good confession. None of these could feature in any performance review or appraisal. In many ways my role is to waste time with students; to be with them and alongside them. This work, in the main, has no immediate visible effects.

This reminds me of a homily I heard many years ago. I cannot remember the preacher, but they said that as Christians we are not called to be successful, we are called to be faithful. I wonder what would happen if I identified one of my targets this year as to just be faithful?

This lunchtime the Mass was celebrated for the uncle of a student who had died. The student came to Mass and we prayed for her and the whole family at this time. During the homily I displayed a picture of Jesus with the caption 'Look Busy Jesus is Watching!' This related to the Gospel of today which contained the advice,

> But know this that if the householder had known at what hour the thief was coming, he would have been awake and would not have left his house to be broken into. You also must be ready; for the Son of man is coming at an hour you do not expect. (Luke 12:39-40)

I didn't preach a homily, as such, but asked those present to think about what it means to look busy for Jesus.

End of round one – *Friday 24th October*

Mass this morning was offered for a young carer who was also present at the Mass. We sang a new song which we practised with the form group beforehand and this seemed to be well received. At lunchtime I met with a group of students in the library who are working with another member of staff to establish a Pax Christi group. It is good when these things develop and reminds me that there are others who are helping to drive and develop chaplaincy in the school. In an ideal situation, chaplaincy is a responsibility of the whole staff not just the chaplain. Today was the last day of this half-term and so we finish today for one week. I am due to go to Norfolk tomorrow with my family.

CHAPTER TWO

Autumn Term –
Leading up to Christmas

31st Week in Ordinary Time

Building bridges – *Monday 3rd November*
(Commemoration of the Faithful Departed – All Souls)

To mark All Souls' Day we offered Mass this morning for all those connected with the school community who have died. Throughout November we place a petition box in front of the altar in which students and staff can place the names of those who have died. By the end of the month the box is always full.

During the morning I had a telephone call from a colleague in another school who wanted some advice. He regularly rings me for support and mentorship. A teacher in his school who is a Muslim had expressed concerns about taking his class to church and was refusing to go. This was causing some bad feeling and meant that a cover teacher was needed whenever the class was due to attend. This particular school is next to the parish church and classes of children and their teachers attend this Mass as part of the timetable. I had experienced a similar situation in the past in a school that I am connected to and was able to give some advice and help in my colleague's own reflection of the situation.

I can understand to some extent where the Muslim teacher is coming from, but it seems a little intolerant. In my own school I never expect staff to pray, genuflect, sing or do anything that may make them feel uncomfortable. However, it would be my hope that anyone who as part of their work needs to come to Mass should do so. It is acceptable for staff to absent themselves from voluntary masses, but I am not sure how I feel about staff choosing to not support a class that they are timetabled to be with. According to my colleague this is the first time that such a request has been made but it does raise the issue of what it means to sign a contract which requires members of staff to support the faith-life of the school. What about principled atheists? What about the indifferent? Once we make concession for a person from one faith or philosophical viewpoint will others also seek to absent themselves from the Catholic activities in the school?

This evening I rang a friend of mine who is an Imam and spoke about the whole thing with him. In Catholic schools we hope that we teach our students to be tolerant citizens. To say that I am not doing something that is important to the foundation of the school does seem to me to be modelling intolerance. I would like to think that if I worked in a Muslim school, I would be happy to attend Friday prayers if it was part of my work, even though I may not join in fully. My friend the Iman agreed and said that if someone chooses to work in a Christian school then they should respect and support the life and foundation that exists whilst maintaining the integrity of their own beliefs and values.

I feel for my colleague and the dilemma that he has been placed in. Catholic schools should be places where all feel welcome and where there is space for dialogue. It is hard to have such dialogue when the other person has made such a clear and definitive stand. This raises the question of what a Christian view of other faiths should be and how this is incorporated into a Catholic institution.

St Thomas Aquinas speaks of other faiths, sciences and philosophies as containing 'seeds of the word'. He argues that many faiths have aspects of the truth and as Jesus is the ultimate expression of truth, the truths found in other faiths find a home in him. This understanding allows us to be generous in our dialogue with those of other faiths and no faith, without compromising our own belief in the uniqueness of Jesus. I can recognise the truths that exist in a Muslim colleague's faith and don't feel threatened by what he or she believes. I do wonder what he thinks the consequences are of him attending Mass. What does he think will happen to him?

As chaplains we should be able to play a significant role in bringing people together in situations such as these. Jesus came to bring unity and to build the bonds of peace between individuals and human communities.

Welcomers – *Wednesday 5th November*

This morning, as I arrived to celebrate Mass, I found that two students had propped open the doors and set up a stand with all the Mass and song booklets on. They were handing the booklets out to those attending and telling them to genuflect as they entered the chapel. The difficulty is that the chapel porch is so cramped and they did cause some congestion. One of the students told me that he had visited his parish at the weekend and saw that they had Welcomers who handed out the books. He said that they had decided to start doing this and had abandoned our previous arrangement where the books are placed on the seats beforehand. I was informed by this enthusiastic pair that what we did before was no good! I am glad that they are taking a lead and responsibility for the chapel but I carefully said that they need to ask first before changing things that we do.

Nobody is going to make their fortune in school chaplaincy. The role is very much a vocation and there are many inspirational lay and ordained chaplains that I know who work tirelessly for very little remuneration. There is a fairly high turnover of lay chaplains and I am sure this is partly the reason. I thought of some of my loyal colleagues in other schools as I read the Gospel at Mass today,

> Whoever does not bear his own cross and come after me, cannot be my disciple. For which of you, desiring to build a tower, does not first sit down and count the cost, whether he has enough to complete it? Otherwise, when he has laid a foundation, and is not able to finish, all who see it begin to mock him, saying, 'This man began to build, and was not able to finish.' Or what king, going to encounter another king in war, will not sit down first and take counsel whether he is able with ten thousand to meet him who comes against him with twenty thousand? And if not, while the other is yet a great way off, he sends an embassy and asks terms of peace. So therefore, whoever of you does not renounce all that he has cannot be my disciple. (Luke 14:27-33)

Bind us together – *Friday 7th November*

In my outside supervision session today I reflected about the member of staff in my colleague's school who refused to come to Mass with his form group and also about staff in general who try not to engage. Insisting that staff come to Mass as part of their contract may be self-defeating but I am also worried about the possibility of a domino effect with some other staff. Sustaining and developing what we do in Catholic schools requires the cooperation and commitment of all the staff to ensure that everything flourishes as it should.

These incidents can create defensiveness on our part which may be unhelpful and destructive. In schools, as staff responsible for Catholic life, if we get into the mentality whereby we feel we need to defend our religion we are actually making God appear to be smaller than he actually is. God does not require us in our fallibility to defend Him. Catholic truth should be proclaimed in a Catholic school but this proclamation should never become defensive and narrow. This is difficult as in school much of our dialogue with staff and students is apologetic and so naturally provides a defence and promotion of the Catholic faith. Achieving unity does require risk-taking. Recognising that God is larger than our divisions can become a starting point for us letting go of our need to become entrenched, otherwise our feelings can contribute to the development a siege mentality.

32nd Week in Ordinary Time

In sympathy – *Monday 10th November (St Leo the Great)*

Most of the staff in Catholic schools are very dedicated professionals who care about their subject and the students they teach. Despite this, over the years in a number of schools, I have come to the conclusion that a large minority are not all that supportive of the Catholic life. I know of teachers who do not pray with their form groups at the start of the day and there are staff members who will avoid liturgical events if at all possible. This makes developing the faith-life of a school more difficult and undermines the whole foundation. Students spot immediately when staff are lukewarm and this then creates a cycle of apathy which is hard to reverse.

Many staff are sympathetic to the faith of the school but this isn't the gift that it first appears. Being sympathetic is not transformative. Jesus calls us to be dynamic and intentional disciples who can bring healing and change to our world. The Gospel has never been advanced by people being sympathetic to it, but only by people who seek to follow Jesus. Part of the life of a Catholic school is to be proclamatory. Values of trust, respect, kindness and honesty are inspiring but without being rooted in the death and resurrection of Jesus, such values are no different from those of a good secular school. We speak so much of distinctiveness in the Catholic sector but we stand to lose something special if the Church doesn't take seriously the need to foster vocations to the teaching profession. There are many outstanding non-Catholic staff in schools who work hard to support the faith-life but having committed and practising Catholic staff does make a real difference. How can we in Catholic schools help people to really catch this vision? Is the system sustainable in the longer term? I once shared this thought with someone senior within the education service and it was as if I had expressed a heresy. Being the product of a Catholic school, I am passionate about the Church's mission in education but equally I am determined that we should aim for high standards in order for our schools to flourish in an increasingly secular age.

Our schools should be 'Beacons of Transformation'. We need Catholics who are prepared to be agents of this transformation.

St Leo the Great (d. 461) who we remembered today was a man of great steadfastness. He worked tirelessly during his papacy for the consolidation of the Church's organisation and held firm when outside pressure seemed to be overwhelming. We need that same courage and determination today if our Catholic schools are to survive. Just as St Leo consolidated the Church's organisation do we need to do the same? Can we sustain the Catholic schools that we have or do we need to close some in order to prune the vine?

Rehearsing the skits – *Wednesday 12th November (St Josaphat)*

This morning I gathered together all the students who have volunteered to participate in the school carol service which always takes place on the last day of the autumn term before we break up for Christmas. In previous years I had been disappointed with my efforts with the carol service as the format was determined and constrained by the musical programme. There was little flexibility and it seemed quite stolid. I felt more like a compère of the music rather than a priest leading those present in worship. Students themselves had also reflected similar feelings to me.

This year, due to staff absence, I had a much freer hand and so, with the Chaplaincy Council, have devised a service with a mixture of traditional carols, Bible readings, drama, humour and several video clips, including a 'Rap Nativity'. We have included a play based on *The Fourth Wise Man* and I have managed to convince some of the students involved in amateur dramatics to take part. To conclude the service, after the final blessing, we have included a few secular Christmas songs to be sung. On these occasions, I always worry about what my more traditional clergy colleagues would think.

I have written a two-man play, which I have called *Tripadvisor Nativity*. It is based on the story of the Nativity through Tripadvisor reports about the Inn in Bethlehem. It is a fun take on the Nativity story but also has an important message. I plan to play the role of the arrogant innkeeper myself, whose character I have based on Al Murray's *Pub Landlord* sketches. After the rehearsal one student tried to persuade me to tone down some of the jokes about other school staff as he was worried that I might get the sack. It was a fun morning with lots of laughter but not as much rehearsing happened as I would have liked.

At the lunchtime Mass today the Gospel reading was the story of the Ten Lepers from Luke's Gospel,

> And as he entered a village, he was met by ten lepers, who stood at a distance and lifted up their voices and said, 'Jesus, Master, have mercy on us.' When he saw them he said to them, 'Go and show yourselves to the priests.' And as they went they were cleansed. Then one of them, when he saw that he was healed, turned back, praising God with a loud voice; and he fell on his face at Jesus' feet, giving him thanks. Now he was a Samaritan. Then said Jesus, 'Were not ten cleansed? Where are the nine? Was no one found to return and give praise to God except this foreigner?' And he said to him, 'Rise and go your way; your faith has made you well.' (Luke 17:12-19)

In the homily I gave examples of when I had not thanked God and when my prayers become more like shopping lists than an encounter with our loving Father. I am the worst person to preach about this as I often overlook all the blessings that God has given me.

Today we offered Mass for a parent who has just been diagnosed with cancer, which was emotional as it was her children who had arranged to have the Mass said.

In whose name? – *Friday 14th November*

During Mass this morning we prayed for all those who have died. It was moving that so many pupils had the courage to mention names of family members and others they had known. Death is a difficult issue to discuss in school and if it were not for November being the month of All Souls I may never have really discussed death at all. Using the Church calendar in school continually reminds me of how important the Church's year and lectionary are. The cycling of the Church year ensures that we think of the more difficult aspects of the faith and life as well as the joyful. This is a safeguard against sanitising our faith and image of God. It also prevents the pet concerns and preoccupations of the chaplain dominating the worship and preaching. The Church's year also makes things easier for me. I can come up with new ideas more easily when I have a framework within which to work and the calendar gives me such a framework. I am always surprised that on many occasions the readings of the day speak into the situations that I find myself in at a particular time. Without the Church's year I think I would be more inclined to portray the Gospel in my own image and not in God's. As St Augustine said, 'If you take what you like from the Gospel and add what you like, it is not the Gospel, it is yourself.' I always need to heed this warning.

33rd Week in Ordinary Time

Halcyon days – *Monday 17th November*

Today was quiet and gave me the opportunity to do some housekeeping jobs which I rarely get the opportunity to do properly. I tidied the sacristy and ordered some more items that we need for the chapel. Often the sacristy resembles a jumble sale or a teenager's bedroom and so it was good to have time today to try to tidy things up a little. I am always picking albs off of the floor and trying to make the altar servers tidy up after themselves. Clergy in parishes take for granted the role of the sacristan but in school I am responsible for this myself. A student is nominated as a sacristan but they do need a lot of support. Whilst this work is neither exciting nor meaningful, it still forms an important part of the unseen work of a school chaplain and needs to be done for the smooth running of the chaplaincy.

Mass this morning was offered for a pupil whose brother has a disability. We prayed that he may grow in strength and we also remembered his parents and those who care for him.

Current affairs – *Wednesday 19th November*

As part of my aim to increase my presence within the Sixth Form Centre, I started running a current affairs group in September. This is one of the activities on offer within an enrichment programme which aims to give students experiences in addition to those offered by the curriculum. We meet once each fortnight and discuss any news items that have interested us. I buy a range of newspapers and we also look at blogs and online content. This also gives me an opportunity to keep up-to-date and I now pay more attention to what is going on in the world during the week so that I can more ably lead this group. I write on a freelance basis for mainly Catholic newspapers and magazines and so this is something that interests me. This group also gives me a platform to get to know some more of the students in a less religious environment. I often feel compartmentalised by students and staff who view me as the religious person and don't see me as anything else. The students who have enrolled are largely ones that I would not have many dealings with and so this has been a positive step.

Today we looked at various newspapers and publications and tried to identify their political biases from the articles that we read. It amazes me that many of the students who are seventeen or eighteen know so little about world events and politics. They have an in-depth knowledge of celebrity gossip but things that really matter are a mystery. These are some of the brightest students, many of whom were straight-A students at GSCE level. Most of the group admit to never watching the news on television, reading newspapers or using the internet to access news. I have reflected whether I would have been the same at their age – I probably was.

Prize-giving – *Thursday 20th November*

We welcomed back tonight students and their parents and carers who left in the summer. Some have continued into the Sixth Form but others have gone on to vocational courses and apprenticeships in other schools, colleges and workplaces. It is always lovely to celebrate achievements and service to the school as well as to catch up with what past students are now doing.

I started the evening with a prayer and then read this well-known prayer by St Teresa of Avila, which I felt had an important message for those present:

> Christ has no body but yours,
> No hands, no feet on earth but yours,
> Yours are the eyes with which he looks
> Compassion on this world,
> Yours are the feet with which he walks to do good,
> Yours are the hands, with which he blesses all
>   the world.

Yours are the hands, yours are the feet,
Yours are the eyes, you are his body.
Christ has no body now but yours,
No hands, no feet on earth but yours,
Yours are the eyes with which he looks
Compassion on this world.
Christ has no body now on earth but yours.

(St Teresa of Avila, 1515–1582)

The keynote speaker tonight was Rosie Goodwin, an alumnus of St Thomas More School, now in her fifties. She is an historical novelist and has written over twenty books. She shared with us her life story. Rosie started life working as a support worker and later developed a career in social services after completing her teacher training. Writing developed later in life and now she is very well known. She is now one of the two hundred and fifty most borrowed library authors in Britain. Her message was important as she told of the importance of hard work and perseverance. Her life also speaks of a journey which has had many twists and turns. Not everyone finds their vocation straight away and some people have several manifestations of their vocation. People develop at different ages and life experiences and maturity opens for us new possibilities. After her talk Rosie presented the prizes and exam certificates.

I had nominated a student for the Catenian Prize for supporting the religious life of the school and was delighted to see that he received nine prizes in total, which were all deserved. He is a lovely young person and I am glad that he chose to stay on in the Sixth Form. He has supported the Catholic life since I have been working in the school and has been key to improving the music. Nothing is too much trouble and he has helped other students to gain the confidence to perform in public, which is essential, as it will not be that long until he leaves to go on to university.

A challenge in school chaplaincy is that a fifth of the community leaves each year. Students become committed, skilled and confident and then move on. I am always therefore trying to spot new students who can be nurtured to take on roles and work alongside older students. We have to keep moving just to stand still. Each Wednesday at Mass we pray for former students and I will certainly remember this year group in my prayers.

Remembering the dead – *Friday 21st November (The Presentation of the Blessed Virgin Mary)*

There were no students in school today as it was a training day. At the November training day we always celebrate a Requiem Mass for all departed staff and family members of the present staff team. This occasion is often charged with emotion and there were several teary eyes in the room today.

I spoke about how people of faith place their grief in a cosmically wider context. This is something which distinguishes a Christian funeral from a secular one. Without faith we only have an end; brokenness and emptiness are sure to follow. In the homily I discussed about how New Atheism often builds 'Aunt Sallies' in order to demolish an image of God and the hope that we have in the resurrection. Many philosophical atheists challenge a view of God who is *Ens Summum* (the Highest Being) but we don't see God in this way and so the arguments are meaningless. St Thomas Aquinas speaks of a God who is *Ipsum esse Subsistens* (the very act of being itself). This is important because we don't see God as the biggest, the greatest, the best, the strongest, or even the oldest being. Rather he is everything and in everything. This is the God who in Exodus 3:14 responds to Moses by saying, 'I am who I am.' God is beyond our imagination. He is who he is. So to pose questions about who created God is really a non-starter.

Atheism places the concept of God and humanity as being in conflict. John Paul Sartre claims that it is not possible to be free and have God. But we cannot be in conflict with a God who is the very essence of being itself. In contrast to atheism's assertions, St Irenaeus declares that 'the Glory of God is a human being fully alive'. God is therefore glorified when we are truly free and in communion with him. I concluded by saying that in our grief and sorrow we should not narrow our image of God to *Ens Summum* but allow ourselves to be swept into the loving arms of the God who is *Ipsum esse Subsistens*.

In place of the Prayers of the Faithful, I invited those present to light candles and pray for the souls of their own loved ones and former colleagues. During this time of reflection there was just some gentle background music which was played on piano. I always find this moving. The staff all light candles but some found it a little too much. This made me contemplate whether this was the right approach. Am I really providing staff with an outlet to express their grief and pray for the departed or am I just exposing them to uncomfortable and difficult emotions? I never want to hurt staff by doing this sort of thing and only wish to help them and give a sense of hope. I will have to talk to a few people over the next few weeks and ask what they think before I do this again.

34th Week in Ordinary Time

Registering – *Monday 24th November*
(St Andrew Dung Lac and his companions)

Today was one of those occasions which were filled with so much activity but by the final bell there was very little to show for it. In the morning I celebrated Mass, led an assembly and then the rest of the day was filled with paperwork. I did the important job of renewing my social work registration with the Health Care Professions Council. I have not practised as a social worker in a statutory capacity for over two years but I continue to maintain my registration. Aspects of my school work and the training that I receive allow me to maintain my professional status. In my work I do use a lot of my experience and skills in social work and the school are keen for me to continue to be registered.

I do feel that being a social worker is enormously helpful and gives different insights, especially as most of my work is with those who struggle with life. Clergy formation takes many forms and I definitely view my social work training and experience as a valuable part of my own formation as a priest.

In school it is always a joy when students really get behind the Catholic life and chaplaincy and offer their skills and talents. I am always looking for new musicians, readers, servers and people to fill other roles. Sometimes what a student can offer may only be small. Recently, one boy started reading; he lacked confidence and it has been good to see him develop over the last few months. His offering may be small but his courage and determination are commendable. I was reminded of him and others who offer their time during the Gospel reading at Mass,

> He looked up and saw the rich putting their gifts into the treasury; and he saw a poor widow put in two copper coins. And he said, 'Truly I tell you, this poor widow has put in more than all of them; for they all contributed out of their abundance, but she out of her poverty put in all the living that she had.' (Luke 21:1-4)

The Lord's Prayer – *Wednesday 26th November*

The Lord's Prayer during Mass today was said in Ukrainian. There are a number of pupils whose first language is not English or who have an additional language at home. Last year we celebrated a multilingual Mass for European Languages Day and that went down well, especially with pupils who had another language. Next week we hope to have the Lord's Prayer in Polish and later in Shona. This is helpful to all the students as it reminds them that they belong to a worldwide faith. Most students only see the local church and school as expressions of the Catholic faith and I reflected upon the universality of our Church in the homily.

First thing this morning I met with a member of staff who has asked for some support at this time. This is always part of my work which shall remain unrecorded but I am glad that my efforts with the staff are starting to result in them seeking my support and prayers.

Meetings – *Friday 28th November*

After the Mass this morning I left school to attend a meeting with the Archdiocese of Birmingham in relation to my parish work. I am normally careful not to alter my school days, as I feel consistency is important for the students and staff, but this does happen occasionally.

1st Week of Advent

The washing up – *Monday 1st December*

One of the key aspects of my school ministry is hospitality and in the chaplaincy room I always offer tea and coffee to students who visit me. The downside is that there is no sink in the room and so the cups get left. I am often busy all day and so the crockery can remain in the crates on the shelves longer than they should. Today I noticed that they had begun to take on a life of their own and so managed to convince a group of students to take them all to the staff room for me and wash them up. It amazes me how even the older students get excited about the prospect of visiting the staff room, which has become for them a sort of forbidden territory. I had volunteers fighting for the privilege of removing the mould from the cups just to see this inner sanctum. I think I may suggest saying a lunchtime Mass in the staffroom as I am sure the numbers would double.

At Mass and at lunchtime we light the first candle on the Advent wreath. I also led an assembly for those in Year 7 about Advent, which I entitled, 'Look Busy, Jesus is Coming'. One of the musicians taught those present an Advent song and we ended by praying that this may be a time of preparation. In school we have really lost the season of Advent as the students are just so excited about the prospect of Christmas, the holidays and the gifts that they will receive. The prophetic message of Advent is therefore all the more important.

Repent – *Wednesday 3rd December*
(St Francis Xavier)

Today, apart from Morning Prayer, Exposition of the Blessed Sacrament and Mass, I spent in the confessional. This is always something I feel is worthwhile, partly because it introduces me to a much larger group of students. It is also a privilege to walk alongside young people as they seek to be reconciled with God.

At the beginning of each lesson period I visited an RE classroom and gave a quick introduction and reminder about the sacrament of reconciliation. I then sat in the chapel waiting for pupils to come. This is something that I should do more often and today was to help mark the season of Advent. It is usual for Catholics to make their confession in the run-up to Christmas. All those who came did so voluntarily and there was not a time when I was not with somebody. I am sure that some came to miss part of the lesson but many took it very seriously and were exceptionally honest and reverent.

I have prepared a simple sheet to help students know what to say which contains an examination of conscience. I see it as my role to make the sacrament of reconciliation as easy for the penitent as possible. Many students in school have not been to confession since their First Communion or confirmation and so they really are coming to the sacrament with fresh eyes. I see it as a success when they leave with a smile on their faces.

Non-Catholics are also encouraged to come for prayer, advice and guidance during these sessions and many do so enthusiastically. This is distinct from the Sacrament of Confession but still mostly takes on a confessional nature. For many it is the first time that they have spoken to someone in such an intimate way about their thoughts and feelings. I always conclude by giving a blessing. This is important as often non-Catholic students can feel excluded from much of the life of the Catholic school.

Take up your cross – *Friday 5th December*

So far this term has been particularly wearing. The incident with the social media network postings and the indifference of some of the students has made me feel a little down. There have been so many positives but these seem to have been clouded by my other experiences at the moment. I think this is often the experience of school chaplains, both lay and ordained. We often work without any visible differences being made and so it can be draining.

I have to remind myself that the Christian faith involves sharing sufferings and that we as Christians are not shielded from the more trying aspects of life. Sacrifice and suffering are central to the Christian faith and we speak of taking up our cross but this is harder to accept in reality. Christianity is not a cult of martyrdom, but suffering is an extension and expression of the divine love of God which roots all that we do with the ultimate expression of love at Calvary. We share in the suffering of Jesus, not in some mystical way, but in the everyday experiences of life.

We are called as priests and the whole people of God to be heralds of Jesus who is both crucified and risen. This vocation involves sharing in the joys and sadness of life which form a union with the suffering of Jesus. Ultimately this is expressed in the Mass, which is the summit of priestly ministry. When we celebrate the Eucharist we celebrate Jesus' death and are nourished by his living presence. So the tensions between these two realities run right through our faith from its summit to the depths of our experiences in life.

Our suffering and experiences are nothing compared with what some Christians have to face, but our own struggles are still something that we need to offer up.

2nd Week of Advent

Spiritual direction – *Monday 8th December*
(Solemnity of the Immaculate Conception of the Blessed Virgin Mary)

This morning was full of activity which included, celebrating Mass, leading a Sixth Form assembly and meeting with several students. After the morning break I had a short meeting with all those taking part in the carol service to ensure that all was on track. Things seem to be progressing well but it is clear that I need to make more time to practise the various parts with them. I am so pleased with their enthusiasm and am glad that they are making suggestions which will make the parts more their own.

At lunchtime we had Exposition of the Blessed Sacrament during which we said the Divine Mercy chaplet and concluded with prayers at the statue of Our Lady, it being her feast day. This is something new that we have introduced and one of our Polish students is a very keen advocate of St Faustina and devotion to the Divine Mercy. Many students seem to respond well to prayers such as the rosary and Divine Mercy chaplet. I think this is because the prayers can become a familiar comfort in a world which is often rapid and unpredictable.

I left school earlier this afternoon to visit my spiritual director. This is a person I see several times each year to make my confession, reflect upon my work and prayer life, and talk to about any issues that I face.

Today I reflected upon how my busyness can often push out God and how I use my activity as an excuse to neglect my prayer life. I am married with a young daughter as well as working in the school, working as a hospital chaplain and in a parish. In the parish I am involved in primary schools, am chair of governors in one school and a foundation governor in the other. In addition, all the usual aspects of parish life feature in my work. I say Mass daily in the parish, even on school days and sometimes keeping all these balls in the air becomes exhausting.

Having a spiritual director is essential for all those in ministry but especially for those who work in schools. Many chaplains, especially lay chaplains, work in isolation and the need to reflect and offload in a spiritual environment cannot be underestimated. I am part of a staff team and receive a great deal of support from my colleagues but as a chaplain there is so much which you carry on your own.

In most schools there is only one chaplain and so life can be lonely at times. If we neglect the spiritual aspect of our work, then what we can often be left with is a sort of shallow secular activism. We try to do things under our own steam and in our own abilities. Such a way of working can achieve a great deal but will never bear as much fruit as a work which is undergirded with prayer and prompted by the Holy Spirit. It is brave to devote more time to prayer and less time to being active, as the world, especially the world of school, is so full of expectations to perform and deliver in a particular way. Prayer is not some sort of specialised activity which is divorced from our work. Rather prayer should be something natural which is rooted in scripture and the sacraments and threaded through all the other aspects of our life experiences. How different would our schools be if chaplains and staff made prayer and worship more of a priority?

Deck the halls – *Wednesday 10th December*

Today was a wet and miserable day. Wet break-times bring their own challenges, which only someone who works in a school can know. Students often become agitated by their confinement indoors and everything gets distracted. We can underestimate the need for young people to get outside, blow away the cobwebs and run off some of their energy.

This afternoon, with the help of several staff I took a group of twenty-five students carol singing to the George Eliot Hospital in Nuneaton, where I also work for a few hours per week as the Catholic chaplain. I have been planning this for some time and had to complete a risk assessment, arrange insurance, gain parental consent as well as help the musicians to learn the carols and Christmas songs that we sang. Arranging any outside trip or event takes so much effort these days.

Three willing students provided the music and the rest of us sang in the Christmas hats that we had brought. For some of the students it was the first time that they had been into a hospital ward and it was a daunting prospect. We started by singing in the main foyer and then were led around the different wards by Rev. Ricarda, the lead chaplain. The most moving part was when we were asked to sing on one of the side bays in the stroke ward. An elderly patient started crying and was really grateful to the students. On some wards we had requests for songs and many patients joined in the singing and applauded us. At one point some of the nursing staff started dancing together which caused some amusement. It was a worthwhile experience and we will definitely try to do it again next year.

These sorts of events are important for many reasons. It helps to build the confidence of the students, gives them a sense of community responsibility, raises awareness of the less fortunate and also reminds them that faith can be fun and compassionate. It is also good for the school as it increases our profile in the community and helps to give a good impression. As a Catholic school, part of our mission should be as a community transforming communities, and so in a small way what we did today was an outliving and expression of this vocation.

The build up to Christmas is always so busy for a school chaplain and there are many additional events to plan and take part in. The words of today's Gospel gave refreshment for my weary mind,

> Come to me, all who labour and are heavy laden, and I will give you rest. Take my yoke upon you, and learn from me; for I am gentle and lowly in heart, and you

will find rest for your souls. For my yoke is easy, and
my burden is light. (Matthew 11:28-30)

Incarnation – *Friday 12th December*

Following the morning Mass, I spent until lunchtime
walking around the school. I visited the IT, technology,
art, library and music departments. I enjoy visiting these
areas and speaking to students and staff about their latest
projects. It is easier to visit these more practical subjects
than some of the classes where my visits would form a
disruption. I always have an opportunity to talk to students
that I never usually meet when out and about on these
occasions and so it is always a positive thing to do. Part of
a chaplain's role should be a visible presence throughout
all of the school. This is an aspect of my work that cannot
easily be measured and yet it is one of the most crucial in
my opinion.

When visiting these departments I often wonder how
the Catholic ethos is lived out and expressed when subjects
do not have an explicit religious faith focus. How do staff
in these areas view the distinctiveness of a school like this?

A trap that we often fall into is viewing the Catholic
life of a school in a very narrow way and in doing so we
restrict our concept of God. The danger of this is that we
perceive that God is only interested in the religious aspect
of human experience and forget that God is the God of
all creation and not just the God of religion. Catholic life
can easily be treated as only the preserve of the chaplaincy
and RE department rather than as the responsibility of the
whole school community. God is the God of the chapel
but also of the technology block, art classroom and the
playground. Our role should be to help students and staff
grow in the realisation of this incarnational truth. Cross-

curricular working with the RE department could be developed more proactively in most schools but we see the imprint of God in all that is creative in life and especially so in the creative aspects of a school's life and curriculum.

Whilst I sometimes question what the wider mission of a Catholic school should be, I can see that having a stake in education ensures that the Church continues to have a platform and role in national life. Schools, like other aspects of the Church's social mission, also ensure that the Church does not recede into some kind of vacuum, becoming preoccupied with the religious dimension of life and thereby diminishing the message and the mystery of the Incarnation.

3rd Week of Advent

Lunchtime – *Monday 15th December*

After the Divine Mercy devotions at lunchtime I joined all those who attended in the chaplaincy room for lunch. It is always good to catch up with students. In school the conversation is often superficial and ranges in all kinds of directions. These occasions help me to keep up-to-date with all that goes on in the lives of the students in our school, their concerns and preoccupations. So much in the lives of young people is fleeting and transient and yet is so important to them. I perceive that the ancient nature of the Catholic faith and its sense of history has a great deal to offer our society with its often superficial outlook, which is limited by the constraints of the present.

Go and make disciples – *Wednesday 17th December*

For some reason at Mass today there were very few communicants and yet the chapel was still reasonably full.

This is something that I have noticed developing over the last year. A number of students are very committed to the life of the chapel but are not Catholic. Most also do not belong to any other Church and many are not baptised into any tradition. Today I gave more blessings than Holy Communion.

Several weeks ago I gathered some of these pupils together to see if there was any way that I could support them. I suggested whether they would like more non-Eucharistic worship. I was taken aback when a number of them said that they did not like the non-Eucharistic worship that we have as much as they enjoy the Mass. One girl said she appreciated and valued the familiarity of the Mass and that she had worked hard to memorise all the responses and words. Many of these students come from hectic backgrounds, and my session with them made me realise that the Mass for them was something which was consistent and stable. Predictability, which often is considered to be something negative, has actually become a gift that has given comfort. Catholic pupils often take the Mass for granted but here were pupils who were discovering it for the first time. Perhaps we inoculate Catholic children against the Mass rather than gradually encouraging them to fall in love with it. Certainly I have found that these non-Catholic children are some of the best supporters of the work that we do. At the end of each term we give certificates to students who have helped to support the Catholic life. This term all of my nominations were for non-Catholics.

The carol service – *Friday 19th December*

Apart from the Mass, the whole day was taken up with setting up and leading the carol service. This year I arranged for the head boy and head girl to lead parts of the service. This was because I was playing the character of the Innkeeper in the play I had written, *Tripadvisor Nativity*. They did a really good job at leading and speaking in front of the whole school, which even some staff prefer not to do. My play went down well and there were lots of laughs at the jokes that I had put into the script. On the screen appeared Tripadvisor reports that I had written about the various visitors to Bethlehem, which told the story of Jesus' birth in a different way. There was one report for Mary and Joseph, one for the Shepherds and another for the Magi. A student acted as the narrator and read the reviews. The Innkeeper was indignant and arrogant. Throughout the carol service different scenes of the play and another play I rewrote based on a play given to me by a friend, *The Fourth Wise Man*, were acted out and this was interspersed with Bible readings, video clips and music. The singing was great and there were lots of smiling faces in the room. I was really pleased that there was a real cross-section of staff and students involved in the readings and the dramas. After I gave the Blessing we sang a few secular Christmas songs.

The carol service always ends the term and the students leave the gymnasium to go home for the Christmas holidays. The staff remained at school for a get-together and also to say farewell to one or two staff members who are leaving today. Everyone else is now finished for a few days but I now have to focus on celebrating Christmas in the busyness of the parish.

CHAPTER THREE

Spring Term – Leading up to February Half-term

Weekdays after Epiphany

Coming together under the Holy Spirit – *Monday 15th January*

In a few weeks the school is due to become part of a multi-academy company with five of the local primary schools. The group will be known as the Academy of the Holy Spirit. Many schools now function as an academy and the Archdiocese of Birmingham has desired for some time that schools join together in this way. Today was a training day and at lunchtime all the staff from the six schools gathered together for a spiritual reflection session.

At the end of the day, Mass was celebrated in the Sixth Form atrium with representatives from the different schools taking part. Fr Michael Glover came to celebrate the Mass and preach but he was losing his voice and so I ended up celebrating the Mass and he gave the homily. Fr Michael is an alumnus of St Thomas More School and two of the primary schools which will form the academy. This was his first time preaching in front of some of his old teachers since his ordination three years ago. He gave an insightful homily about the Holy Spirit and what opportunities could present themselves with having this dedication. It was wonderful to celebrate Mass in such a packed environment and the singing and contribution from all of the staff was fantastic. I was really pleased by the effort that our own staff made in attending the celebration.

Mass is a great way of marking an occasion like this and drawing people together. Sometimes I consider whether a non-Eucharistic service would be more appropriate and accessible to all people, but today there was a tangible sense of unity, purpose and belonging through the celebration.

Chalk – *Wednesday 7th January*

Over the last couple of years we have blessed chalk near to the feast of the Epiphany. It is traditional to bless chalk and mark the names of the three Magi over doors of houses along with the year in numerals. This is as a reminder of God's protection and an invitation for Jesus to be a daily guest in our home and also that our homes should always be a place of welcome. Students seem to like this and most take chalk with them at the end of the service. I just hope that they use it properly.

Our second reading at Mass today reinforced the message behind the chalking. Receiving Jesus ourselves is inextricably linked to loving others and being hospitable as an outpouring of his love,

> Beloved, if God so loved us, we also ought to love one another. No man has ever seen God; if we love one another, God abides in us and his love is perfected in us. By this we know that we abide in him and he in us, because he has given us of his own Spirit. And we have seen and testify that the Father has sent his Son

as the Saviour of the world. Whoever confesses that Jesus is the Son of God, God abides in him, and he in God. So we know and believe the love God has for us. God is love, and he who abides in love abides in God, and God abides in him. In this is love perfected with us, that we may have confidence for the Day of Judgment, because as he is so are we in this world. There is no fear in love, but perfect love casts out fear. For fear has to do with punishment, and he who fears is not perfected in love. (1 John 4:11-18)

The new year has become less meaningful for me than it used to be and this is as a direct consequence of working in a school. The academic year tends to have more of an impact nowadays. I think mostly in terms of the year starting in September and ending in mid-July. The Church year is still important and forms the basis for what I do, yet I divide my year into half-terms, terms and summer holidays. It reminds me that all 'new years' are socially constructed and artificial and yet we place so much importance in them.

Silence? – *Friday 9th January*

As with most Friday celebrations of the Mass, today was fraught beforehand. There were the usual issues with the altar servers and many of the volunteers get impatient and restless as we wait for the form group to arrive. I had to try to calm everyone down and keep a sense of order.

Ideally, as the celebrant I should make time for quiet recollection before and after the Mass. In other contexts, I always manage to create some time before the celebration begins to have prayerful preparation. This is virtually impossible to achieve in school. Celebrating Mass in school becomes far more difficult and I feel guilty that I often approach the altar with such a chaotic interior.

This is something as chaplains we need to be aware of. Whether ordained or lay, chaplains have a huge responsibility in leading worship and helping others to be swept up into the reality of communion with the living God. If we are to do this well, we need to be people who have first prayerfully prepared. Whether it be collective worship in an assembly, an act of worship in the chapel or prayers in the staff room, preparation before the Lord is key. All too often I neglect this and am swept along with the competing demands which are a feature of all schools that I have known.

1st Week in Ordinary Time

Meet the parents – *Monday 12th January*

In a school with a large geographical catchment area it is always a challenge to develop relationships with parents. Many students travel to school on buses and so parents rarely come into contact with the school. Today we celebrated a Mass for parents, carers and supporters. This was a student's idea. He asked me a while ago whether his mother could come and see him in his role as an altar server. From our conversation the idea of inviting all parents to a special Mass developed. For a first attempt I was pleased as a good number of parents and grandparents turned up. We had a range of different music and lots of pupils were involved in some way. Over coffee afterwards I had a good chat with many of the parents and grandparents. One grandmother was so pleased that her grandson was involved in the chaplaincy as his direct family no longer practise the faith. A mother shared with me how she was bemused by her son's current interest in religion but was happy to be proudly supporting him today. It was a worthwhile experience and I hope we can run this sort of event more often.

Historically, Catholic education has worked well because of a three-way relationship between the School, the Family and the local Parish. Families are now very complex and the relationship with the Church is often weak or non-existent. In many families, practice of the faith just doesn't feature high on their list of priorities. They like Catholic schools but what makes them distinctive is largely an irrelevance to their daily lives. They want the fruits but they don't want to be the roots. Without the three-way relationship between school, home and local church things have certainly become more challenging. The increase in dedicated lay chaplaincy is an important way of thinking creatively about the future of our Catholic schools. We need to develop more initiatives to ensure that our schools continue to have a viable future. We certainly cannot rely on old models which relate to a form of family and parish life that no longer exists.

Nuns! – *Wednesday 14th January*

This morning a group of staff and students went in the school minibus to Mater Ecclesiae, a convent in Monks Kirby, near Rugby. We had been asked to lead a session in a day of prayer for vocations to the religious life. The whole day was to be spent in the presence of the Blessed Sacrament and different groups and individuals from the deanery had volunteered to lead half-hour sessions throughout the day.

I have a great affection for Mater Ecclesiae and it was in this convent that I celebrated my first Mass as a Catholic priest. I have continued to offer several masses here each week and know the sisters well. I am always grateful for their constant prayers and support. Mater Ecclesiae was founded in the 1980s as a congregation for late vocations.

Many of the sisters have had careers and some have children and grandchildren.

Most of the day had been silent but our session also included music, readings and poetry. The students themselves had planned what we offered and had written the prayers. The periods of silence were intensified, rather than diminished, because they were surrounded by strong singing. This contrast felt really powerful. Some of the local parishioners looked a little uneasy during some of the more contemporary songs that we sang, but I felt that what we offered brought a sense of reverence and freshness to the day. These sorts of activities help to build the students' confidence and it is always good when they get positive feedback from people outside of the school environment as it has far more impact.

Encroaching musicians – *Friday 16th January*

We are very fortunate at school to have student musicians who are dedicated to playing for nearly all the school masses and liturgies. They keep up-to-date with developments in Catholic music but tend to favour compositions by more evangelical musicians and I have to agree that this sort of music is received very positively by the wider student body. Recently, they have been watching video clips on the internet of musicians playing for worship in large mega-churches such as Vineyard and Hillsong. Some of the students also attend regular youth worship in a local house church and so have experienced this form of music first hand. In these churches the musicians are usually placed centre stage and the main musician is often referred to as the worship leader.

Over the past few weeks I have noticed the musicians moving closer and closer to the altar from their usual position in the music corner, which is just to the side.

Today during the Mass, they gradually moved right into the middle, in front of the altar, emulating the musicians from the evangelical churches that they had been observing. You could tell that the rest of the congregation were a little puzzled as to what was going on. The musicians' dedication is amazing and has been sustained for several years but it is important that the musical life aids the liturgy and does not dominate it.

After Mass I had a meeting with the musicians and discussed this. Gently I explained why in the Mass the altar is the focus and that nothing should detract from the central place of honour given to the altar and the celebration of the sacraments. It is hard to explain to students of mixed ages why one Christian community has one practice and we have another. I think they thought that I was being a bit of a hardliner. I want to continue to support and encourage the enthusiasm of the musicians, but following today's amusing incident I am aware that I may need to develop some liturgical training and awareness of the riches of Catholic worship.

2nd Week in Ordinary Time

This and that – *Monday 19th January*
(St Wulfstan – Diocesan Feast: Archdiocese of Birmingham)

Mass this morning was offered to celebrate the birthday of a staff member's mother. There were a good number present. It astounds me that students still come on a voluntary basis to this early Mass, especially as the mornings are so dark and cold. The chapel was exceptionally cold this morning and the heating only came on after the consecration. At the end of Mass I blessed a new Bible for a student.

At break time a student came up to me in the playground and asked whether I would visit his mother who was in hospital. He was going himself after school and so I agreed to meet him there. I had visited his mother before and although she is not a Catholic she was grateful for the prayers that we offered. I agreed to call again during the week. I find increasingly that I am being called on to do this sort of thing. Over the last few years I have visited grandparents and parents of students who are in hospital. Funerals of students' family members are also something that I have increasingly been asked to do.

During Exposition of the Blessed Sacrament we listened to music which a student had downloaded onto his phone. He had planned it specifically for this time and the music included some Christian worship songs as well as reflective instrumental music. It really was moving the way that he had chosen what to play and the music led us beautifully into the silent time of prayer just before the Benediction.

This afternoon I spent time seeing students on a one-to-one basis. A great deal of time was spent walking through the corridors to collect the students from their lessons and taking them to the chaplaincy room. I often think about how many miles I must walk in a day.

A Eucharistic community? – *Wednesday 21st January (St Agnes)*

We celebrated the memorial of St Agnes at lunchtime today. She was a saint we do not know that much about and her story is largely lost in the mists of time. During the homily we reflected upon the age of St Agnes, who was only twelve years old when she was martyred. Many of the students were surprised that someone who was younger than most of them should have been martyred for her faith. We also prayed for children today, especially in the plain of Nineveh and Syria, who continue to suffer because of religious intolerance and extremism. We offered the Mass for a pupil's family who are caught up in the conflict in Ukraine.

I really feel an attachment to those who come to Mass on a voluntary basis and there is a real bond developing between this group. I was advised when I started work as a school chaplain to not think of the school as my parish and I have always been careful to follow this advice. However, the sense of community amongst the musicians, servers, readers and supporters really has formed over the last few years. Disputes arise and arguments happen and so it is perhaps becoming more like an authentic parish than I care to admit. Despite not being a parish, I have come to the realisation that we are growing in many ways into a real and vibrant Eucharistic community. We celebrate Jesus' presence until he comes again, bring our needs and concerns before him and support each other. When students left at the end of last year there was a real sense of sadness amongst the younger students that some of their number had moved on. For many of the students this is one of the only functional communities that they relate to. I hope that this can develop further and that the students can begin to discover the mystery of the Mass and be moved by the presence of Jesus. There is never a substitute for the local parish and I always encourage students to make links with their own local church communities.

This is something that those who only come to Mass as part of the timetable never experience, as compulsory masses have a completely different feel. At these larger celebrations there is not the sense of intimacy and I wished that a much larger group of students could experience the sense of togetherness and warmth that we have on these more intimate occasions. The whole school and year masses necessarily take on more formality. Pupils have to sit in rows and there is very little opportunity for the interaction and spontaneity that we experience in the voluntary masses. The more formal nature of these larger occasions creates a distance that does not exist in other settings despite my efforts to develop a more relaxed atmosphere.

I do worry what will happen to this community if I leave. I am not planning on going anywhere but I recognise that school chaplaincy will not be for ever. Having a priest employed by a school is very unusual nowadays. The normal pattern is to have a lay chaplain or youth minister working in the school with a local priest visiting to say Mass and celebrate the sacraments. For me relationship is everything and I believe that I would find celebrating Mass in school far more difficult if I didn't know the pupils and see them on a day-to-day basis. I don't envy my clergy colleagues who are chaplains and have to squeeze schools into already busy schedules as parish clergy. I also believe that the behaviour in Mass and conduct of students is improved because they know me and I know them. I do worry that I am building up a form of chaplaincy that is unsustainable but I also couldn't envisage doing what I do outside of the framework of the sacraments.

Once a deacon – *Friday 23rd January*

After Mass this morning I met a number of the pupils that I support on a one-to-one basis for pastoral support. I find that I use my social-work skills so much in these situations and this training and experience has given me a crucial foundation. I often reflect that much of my work has a diaconal character. As a priest, I always remain a deacon and unless I continue to have a deacon's heart and mind I will never be a very good priest.

The appointing of the Twelve by Jesus was today's Gospel. As I read the names I remembered that these were men plucked from obscurity. They never knew that they would be known about throughout the world. It reminds me not to dismiss those who seem weak or on the margins as they could be the next people that Jesus chooses.

> And he went up into the hills, and called to him those whom he desired; and they came to him. And he appointed twelve, to be with him, and to be sent out to preach and have authority to cast out demons: Simon whom he surnamed Peter; James the son of Zebedee and John the brother of James, whom he surnamed Boanerges, that is, sons of thunder; Andrew, and Philip, and Bartholomew, and Matthew, and Thomas, and James the son of Alphaeus, and Thaddaeus, and Simon the Cananaean, and Judas Iscariot, who betrayed him. (Mark 3:13-19)

3rd Week in Ordinary Time

Family tree – *Wednesday 28th January*
(St Thomas Aquinas)

One of the most rewarding aspects of my work is helping students who are going through difficult situations in their lives. Such trauma as family breakdown, bereavement and loss, low self-esteem, anxiety are all things that I encounter during my ministry in schools. Often all I offer is a listening ear and a cup of tea and other times I may use other techniques to help young people make sense of their situation and surroundings.

One method that has helped greatly has been working with students to complete a family tree. This involves, sometimes over several weeks, drawing a family tree which not only lists family members but also identifies the nature of each relationship. A relationship that is strained may be identified by a particular symbol or word. A positive relationship can be marked by a different colour or shading. The aim is to help students to gain a better understanding of family dynamics and their own support networks. Often students struggle to articulate or comprehend how their own family functions and how they relate to it. In most situations I find that completing a family tree helps to develop a greater awareness. It is useful for me as students' families can be so complicated nowadays and seeing everything on paper is far clearer than trying to follow a description. During the completion of the family tree we talk about what is being written down and this also is helpful because it allows students to talk to me about their families without feeling self-conscious.

My work as a chaplain is very distinct from that of a counsellor or social worker. Whilst I rely on my social work background, I see my work very much as priestly. During family-tree work I will talk about the role of faith and spirituality within the family and often this features in the trees that the students draw. I find that including aspects of faith does not pose a barrier unless it is superficial. If faith is woven into the very fabric of the sessions I have with students it seems far more natural. For example, when a student is first referred to me I tell them about myself and what chaplaincy means. I explain that all sessions with me will involve prayer and that I also pray for them as well as work through the various issues. Chaplaincy allows students' concerns to be placed in a larger cosmic context which other forms of intervention cannot do. This then becomes very much part of the healing ministry of the Church.

The Parable of the Sower was the Gospel reading at the Mass (Mark 4:1-20). This is a very well-known parable. In school we sow many seeds and rarely see the fruit of our labours. It is my prayer that one day some of what I do will bear fruit in the lives of these young people.

Under the seal – *Friday 30th January*

The Gospel reading today was the Parable of the Mustard Seed (Mark 4:26-34),

> And he said, 'With what can we compare the kingdom of God, or what parable shall we use for it? It is like a grain of mustard seed, which, when sown upon the ground, is the smallest of all the seeds on earth; yet when it is sown it grows up and becomes the greatest of all shrubs, and puts forth large branches, so that the birds of the air can make nests in its shade.' (Mark 4:26-32)

We at times may not feel like the Kingdom of God has broken into our world. This can be especially true for those in ministry who don't always see the fruits of their labours. I find in today's Gospel reading reassurance that the Kingdom is also in the little things.

Apart from Mass and an hour spent in the Sixth Form Learning Resource Centre (LRC), the day was devoted to hearing confessions. The chapel is not ideal for this, as in order to preserve confidentiality the students have to wait outside in the corridor and so there is a lack of anonymity. Ideally a separate waiting area would be available for them. This was especially noticeable at lunchtime when the corridors are busier and a couple of students commented that it made them felt that waiting outside drew attention to them. In future I may ask if we can use the library as there would be space to wait and a discreet corner which could become the confessional. This would lose some of the feeling that is gained by being in front of the Blessed Sacrament in the chapel, but it would solve some of the problems. I do not want students to be put off because the present arrangements are inadequate.

In most schools, space is a precious commodity but for chaplaincy having dedicated space is essential. We are fortunate to have a distinctive chapel as a sacred sanctuary and the school value and respect this. The chapel is always available and there is never any pressure for it to be used for other purposes. In some schools I know, the chapel has become multi-purpose and the sense of the sacred is lost. I have found that recent investments in our chapel have paid off in terms of students identifying with the space as a place of prayer.

One of the important and underestimated roles of chaplains is the management and development of chapels and prayer rooms. A good and focused environment can lead us into a sense of the sacred and so well-cared-for chapels become important catalysts for evangelisation in our schools.

4th Week in Ordinary Time

Candlemas – *Monday 2nd February*
(Feast of the Presentation of Our Lord in the Temple)

We lit and blessed candles today at Mass as we celebrated the feast of the Presentation of Our Lord in the Temple. At lunchtime we also used candles again as we sang a song which paraphrases the Nunc Dimittis, the song that Simeon sang in Luke's Gospel when Jesus was presented in the Temple:

> Lord, now you are letting your servant depart in peace, according to your word; for my eyes have seen your salvation which you have prepared in the presence of all peoples, a light for revelation to the Gentiles, and for glory to your people Israel. (Luke 2:29-32, *ESVUK*)

A member of staff who is very supportive of the chaplaincy and who comes from an evangelical church asked me why using candles and the other externals is so important. She has grown in appreciation of the Catholic faith since working in the school and is intrigued by many of the things that we do and say. We had a good discussion, which helped me to reflect on things that often I take for granted.

For me, using externals such as candles, is very important when working with young people. I find that such things speak far more powerfully than any homily or reading, which often becomes 'white noise' to a bored teenager. Therefore, on any occasion possible, I get out the holy water, use colour, incense, candles, bells, salt, and chalk. To an outsider it may seem bizarre and ritualistic, even superstitious. For us as humans there is part of our being that longs for something that is tangible. This desire may be something that we cannot explain but using such things gives us what words cannot afford us. I find this particularly important when working with pupils who are less articulate and academically gifted. The candles today remind us of God's light, his goodness and his love for us.

We offered the Mass today for a member of staff who is struggling in school at this time.

This afternoon, I had a telephone call from the mother of a student. His grandmother had died unexpectedly over the weekend and the family are devastated. The student was not in school today but his mother asked if I would see him when he returned. They would like me to lead the funeral service as they know me. We talked about the family's wishes and what the person themselves would have wanted. It became clear that the family did not want a Mass but still wished to have a service that was Catholic. I arranged to visit the family at home and waited for the funeral directors to contact me to confirm the arrangements.

When I began working in schools in never thought that I would have any sort of funeral ministry but over the last few years I have been asked by families to help them through these difficult times in their lives.

Praying the Hours – *Wednesday 4th February*

For some time now I have been saying Morning Prayer from the Breviary during Exposition of the Blessed Sacrament in the school chapel. Students have recently been asking me about this and so today I printed off sheets and we started to pray the Office together. If this works well I may try to get the school to by some proper prayer books for us to use.

At break time I went out onto the playground. Clergy can often worry that they are not busy enough and we fill our diaries with so many commitments that we forget that often having a ministry of availability is more important. Without realising it our obliviously cycling days blend into each other and we become less and less productive. One of the most fruitful parts of my ministry is spent just treading the tarmac and 'wasting time' with students. I can have all sorts of conversations and encounters on the playground. Students will give me prayer requests, ask for appointments, confess their sins, tell a joke, and share their joys and concerns. Being available in this way is fun and unpredictable. Jesus doesn't want ministry to always be pressured and exhausting. He calls us to be who we are in the situations that he leads us into. If we try to work completely under our own strength, we soon become too preoccupied with being industrious and our lives become chaotic. It is then that we stop making space for Jesus to speak to us and through us. We cannot make ourselves holy by our own doing and hard work. Holiness is a gift from God.

The search for meaning – *Friday 6th February*
(St Paul Miki and his companions)

This morning's Mass celebrated the memorial of St Paul Miki and his companions who were martyred in Japan between 1564 and 1566. I started the homily by asking what St Paul Miki and Pope Francis had in common. I knew that nobody would know the answer that I was looking for. I was given many answers! Both were Jesuits and I spoke about the sacrificial life that many Jesuits had lived throughout this period of history and the need for religious tolerance in the world today, starting with ourselves and our own families and communities. Tolerance is always something that we speak about in school. Those with a secular agenda would perceive that Catholic schools are centres of sectarian intolerance but the reality couldn't be further from the truth. Forming good and responsible citizens is very much part of our vocation as a school. Catholic schools are often more ethnically diverse than people realise and students from all faiths and none are welcomed and accepted.

After Mass, I met with a student to help him prepare and think about his funeral reflection, which he will read at his grandmother's funeral on Monday. He is a wonderful young man and although he would say he is not religious, he actually communicates a great deal about faith and hope in what he plans to say at Monday's service. This morning's Mass was offered for him, his grandmother and for the courage to deliver his tribute.

5th Week in Ordinary Time

Saying farewell – *Monday 9th February*

Mass was offered this morning for a member of staff who is finding life difficult at the moment. I announced this as a private intention, as there were students present.

After Morning Prayer and Exposition of the Blessed Sacrament I drove the five-minute journey to the Heart of England Crematorium for the funeral. The family had requested that there be no dark colours and there was a theme of daffodils. It is always a privilege to support families in such situations and I am always aware of the great responsibility that this brings. There is only one opportunity to get things right and this always brings a slight pressure on such occasions. We sang 'All Things Bright and Beautiful' and the student read his recollection with feeling and love. He managed to ensure that there was not a dry eye in the room. We ended with a song by James Blunt, during which everyone left the chapel. I stayed outside for a while and chatted to members of the family and congratulated the student on his bravery.

In situations such as these I tend to stick fairly lightly to the Church's liturgy. Often, the words that we use and the prayers that we say assume a level of faith and commitment which is simply not there. What does it mean to place a Bible on someone's coffin and say that the person treasured the words in their life when they didn't even own a Bible? What does this communicate to the family when they know that faith played almost no role in their loved one's life? What message do we give when the Church says 'no' to families' requests during this time when their hearts are breaking?

Over time I have developed the view that it is better to be gently honest than to celebrate something which wasn't true. I have been to too many funerals which were so full of half-evasions and partial truths that the departed becomes so unrecognisable. I feel grasping honesty brings a greater integrity than merely pretending that things were different, and also does more justice to the Christian Faith and to the memory of the person. Ultimately this opens up further possibilities in a situation where sharing the love of Jesus in the brokenness is more important than rigidly following the rules. For most people in that chapel today, the Catholic Church has become an irrelevance, and even for those who are Catholics much of the language and prayers have developed a certain ambiguity. The family, whom I know, are all good, honest and hardworking people but they are unfamiliar with the great story of God's love for the world. The faith which animates me and gives hope to my own mortal existence has long faded from the forefront of their minds.

The family did want a Catholic funeral and asked me to be the celebrant and so there obviously is some foundation somewhere. This may have been because of the connection with the school and also knowing me. Despite this, it is a big thing to have a secular funeral and to say that this is 'the end'. Setting human life in the context of something that is far larger than we are is important. Some may say that it is about 'keeping options open' or following cultural norms but I would like to think that it is a recognition of that spark of faith, that tiny flame, which deep down exists in us all.

The family were appreciative of the service, and I arranged to see Tom on Wednesday in school. He really did a superb job. It is very courageous at his age to read something so intimate in the presence of his closest family.

This afternoon was spent hearing confessions in the chapel. In an afternoon I can hear up to forty confessions and I always feel privileged to have gained the trust of the students who share their deepest thoughts, emotions and concerns with me. Hearing confessions also allows me to meet with a much larger number of pupils than my work normally permits. This is very much a hidden part of a priest's work and in school it is the only place where complete confidentiality is guaranteed. By the end of the day I was shattered. Hearing confessions is one of the most tiring things that I have to do as a priest, although it is also the most rewarding.

Duelling guitars – *Wednesday 11th February*
(Our Lady of Lourdes)

After the simple prayers in chapel this morning, I met with a student. We meet once each week and play the guitar together. We have been doing this for some time now. He is someone who finds school difficult and is a more practical person than academic. I was asked to support him and introduced him to the guitar when it became apparent that he was not comfortable with talking and sharing his thoughts and feelings. Learning chords on the guitar has given a focus to our meetings. We chat and play music from chord sheets which he chooses and downloads from the internet. We have discussed more meaningful matters during these sessions than we ever would have done if we had met in more a more conventional way. This is not deceitful and I have always made it clear to him that our sessions have a specific purpose. I have never been a very good guitarist and now he is much better than I am and so the master has become the pupil.

Doing what God asks is difficult, yet as Christians we should be constantly discerning what we are called to do and be. A school chaplain can easily fill his or her day with so much busyness and never be doing what Jesus is calling us to do. The miracle of the Wedding at Cana was our Gospel reading for Mass today. In it Our Lady is clear when she instructs the servants, 'Do whatever he tells you.'

> When the wine failed, the mother of Jesus said to him, 'They have no wine.' And Jesus said to her, 'O woman, what have you to do with me? My hour has not yet come' His mother said to the servants, 'Do whatever he tells you.' Now six stone jars were standing there, for the Jewish rites of purification, each holding twenty or thirty gallons. Jesus said to them, 'Fill the jars with water.' And they filled them up to the brim. He said to them, 'Now draw some out, and take it to the steward of the feast.' So they took it. When the steward of the feast tasted the water now become wine, and did not know where it came from (though the servants who had drawn the water knew), the steward of the feast called the bridegroom and said to him, 'Every man serves the good wine first; and when men have drunk freely, then the poor wine; but you have kept the good wine until now.' This, the first of his signs, Jesus did at Cana in Galilee, and manifested his glory; and his disciples believed in him. (John 2:3-11)

Making time in a busy school day to try listen to the prompting of the Holy Spirit is almost impossible. Even if time is set aside it will often be disrupted by pupils or other demands on our time. Yet for all chaplains, regular reflection is ever important, otherwise we will find it hard to respond to the command Our Lady gave at Cana.

I had a long chat with a member of staff today when I collected my photocopying from her. She does so much for me in the chaplaincy and I really would have a much heavier workload if she was not so ready to help and encourage me in all that I do. I am very fortunate that a number of staff support my work in these kinds of ways. As a chaplain it is important to work alongside colleagues who are willing to become involved in the Catholic life of the school.

Blessing – *Friday 13th February*

Today at Mass we heard about the healing and restorative power of Jesus,

> Then he returned from the region of Tyre, and went through Sidon to the Sea of Galilee, through the region of the Decapolis. And they brought to him a man who was deaf and had an impediment in his speech; and they besought him to lay his hand upon him. And taking him aside from the multitude privately, he put his fingers into his ears, and he spat and touched his tongue; and looking up to heaven, he sighed, and said to him, 'Ephphatha,' that is, 'Be opened.' And his ears were opened, his tongue was released, and he spoke plainly. And he charged them to tell no one; but the more he charged them, the more zealously they proclaimed it. And they were astonished beyond measure, saying, 'He has done all things well; he even makes the deaf hear and the dumb speak.' (Mark 7:31-37)

School ministry may not obviously be viewed as part of the healing ministry of the Church. Over the last few years I have begun to see my role and the role of schools increasingly in the context of healing. In school we work with so many young people who are broken or emotionally wounded in some way. Divorce, separation, low self-esteem, self-harm, neglect and abuse are all realities that chaplains will encounter in schools. Sometimes the student's school and its staff will be the only stable aspect of their life. This presents a major responsibility on the part of the school chaplain, who many students will look to for support and guidance.

It is necessary that school chaplains and lay chaplains are equipped with the knowledge, skills and experience to deal with complex situations. Part of the problem is the lack of resourcing of chaplaincy. This is something that the wider Church needs to grasp. Lay chaplaincy is still in its infancy and models and patterns of ministry are still lacking in many places. With the reduction over time of practising Catholic staff, school chaplaincy is going to be more important than ever in promoting the values of the Kingdom and the faith-life of our communities.

After Mass this morning, a couple of pupils stayed behind so that I could bless some items for them. This is a fairly new and growing part of my ministry and has developed completely unexpectedly. Items that are brought can range from religious items to a new pencil case, watch or mobile phone. Today it was rosary beads and a new crucifix necklace. I placed the items on the altar and said a prayer of blessing using Holy Water. I am becoming increasingly aware that the physicality of such sacramentals are important in my ministry and help the students engage with something deeper. It is good that this has been an aspect that has developed directly from the requests of students themselves.

It was the last day of the half-term. I am having a few days away with my family and visiting my brother in Ipswich. It has been a busy half-term and I have been counting down to this week of respite.

Mass today was offered for a student's mother who has a job interview early next week.

CHAPTER FOUR
Spring Term – Lent

1st Week of Lent

Lent – *Monday 23rd February*
(St Polycarp)

This was the beginning of first week of Lent. Ash Wednesday fell during the half-term break which gave me great relief. Normally, I have to lead six liturgies back to back for Ash Wednesday as each year group have their own time of worship. By the end my voice is croaking from singing and speaking the same things six times over. My thumb is usually numb from drawing the ash crosses on hundreds of oily foreheads.

At Mass this morning there were a good number present. Mass was offered for the soul of a pupil who died two years ago at around this time. It reminded me of an extremely difficult period in the school and one which placed a great emotional demand upon me at the time. It was during my first year as a school chaplain, and despite my previous work as a social worker and in parishes, I was still inexperienced and finding my feet. I was involved in supporting his family members who were pupils in the school and working with his class and year group to mark this tragic event. Concelebrating his funeral Mass in the packed church was a real privilege and honour and later we celebrated several requiem masses in school. The Processional Cross in the chapel was presented in his memory and we used it this morning. For many of the students it was the first time they had experienced the death of someone that they knew closely and reminded them starkly of their own mortality. There was a massive mixture of emotions at the time. So we offered the Mass and prayed for his soul and also for his family and friends.

Today was the feast of St Polycarp, Bishop of Smyrna, who was martyred in AD 155. Polycarp was the name that I chose when I was confirmed and received into the Catholic Church. Today I told the story of St Polycarp during the homily. He was an elderly man and a renowned and faithful bishop who remained defiant to the end despite the opportunity to recant his faith. The story of his martyrdom is greatly embellished but his life today reminds us that even in frailty we can serve God faithfully.

The seminarian – *Wednesday 25th February*

A seminarian, Joshua, came to visit the school this morning. I always enjoy sharing my work with others and having students and visitors. Today I saw the school in a different and fresh way. It was a bit like showing a foreign visitor around your home town and learning new things at the same time. Joshua asked important questions which made me think about my work more deeply and he made some interesting observations and comments about the school and my ministry.

For many seminarians visiting a school during their placements is often the first time they have been in school since they left school themselves. Schools are such a big part of the life and ministry of a Catholic priest and yet so little time is spent during training to help seminarians understand the complex world of education. After ordination, priests are expected to have a role in school governance, understand the culture and jargon of schools and act as chaplains. More often than not they are completely thrown in at the deep end.

The rest of the day was spent taking Joshua around various religious education lessons where the pupils quizzed him on a range of topics. We discussed celibacy, pay, private life, sense of vocation, motivation, sex and family. One boy in a Year 9 class asked about married priests, knowing that I am married. Another asked about what happens if you no longer want to be a priest. I enjoy these question-and-answer sessions as they help me to sharpen my own thoughts, ideas and opinions, but they are exhausting. Joshua seemed to enjoy his day in school.

School Saints – *Friday 27th February*
(St Margaret Clitherow, St Anne Line and
St Margaret Ward)

Today was the school's memorial of St Margaret Clitherow, St Anne Line and St Margaret Ward. Margaret Clitherow, after whom one of our school houses is named, was martyred for her faith on Good Friday 1586 by being crushed to death. She was a convert to Catholicism and was arrested for protecting and hiding priests. In the homily I told the story of St Margaret and also that of a modern-day martyr, reflecting that there are still those in the world who are forced to die for the faith that we ignore or take for granted. It is sad that we hear so little about the persecuted Christians in the media.

Today another member of staff gave me a passage from scripture to reflect on. It is from John's Gospel:

> I am the vine, you are the branches. He who abides
> in me, and I in him, he it is that bears much fruit, for
> apart from me you can do nothing. (John 15:5)

I have been reflecting upon this all day. I am guilty of being so busy doing 'holy' things that I forget to personally include Jesus in what I am doing. Finding time for Jesus in a busy school is difficult and yet I know deep down that action without prayer is fruitless. I support others to be contemplative but completely neglect my own inner life. Only when we are rooted in God's love through prayer can we carry the burdens of our work and ministry. I expect my own strength and abilities to give me what only Jesus can deliver. This is compounded by the nature of school chaplaincy where often you can feel the burdens of ministry without seeing the fruits of your labours.

This afternoon I had an appointment with a member of staff who is struggling at this time. We talked for over an hour and a half and prayed together. I have been praying for some time about my role in supporting staff and things now seem to be coming together.

2nd Week of Lent

Planning for Vocations Day – *Monday 2nd March (St Chad)*

During Exposition and Morning Prayer, I led a short meditation on today's Gospel reading which was the story of the Transfiguration from Mark's Gospel. We did not read this at Mass as in the Archdiocese of Birmingham it is the feast of St Chad and so I was glad to take the opportunity to use the feria reading in a different context. In the meditation we reflected upon the glorious image of Jesus' transfiguration contrasted with the shameful scene of Calvary. One cannot be fully understood without the other. I found preparing this and leading this meditation had deepened my understanding of Jesus' passion. I often find that I am spiritually fed myself when I prepare to lead activities and plan to give homilies.

Today a few of us went to a meeting with Chris, who works for the Vocations Service within the Archdiocese of Birmingham, to plan Vocations Day. This event is something that we run every year for students in Year 9. It is a day which is meant to be a time of reflection upon what our vocation in life is. We do not focus narrowly on vocation and think purely of priests and religious, but rather we aim to focus upon the purpose of life and what Jesus has planned for every one of us.

Over the last few years I have found that the pattern that I inherited has been lacking in some aspects. Vocations Day has taken place within school and a visiting youth team have come in to facilitate the day for us. The youth team always did a good job but there was not much impact as it largely felt like another school day. This year I had the idea of taking Vocations Day out of school and visiting St Mary's College, Oscott, the seminary for the Archdiocese of Birmingham. Hopefully going to a dramatic building, which is a strong centre of formation and vocational discernment, will have more of an impact upon this year's students. We discussed what the day should look like and hope to be able to take as many Year 9 students as possible. Some seminarians from Oscott and some Dominican friars from Blackfriars in Oxford have agreed to help and so this should give the day a good foundation. I am hoping to get a friend who is a doctor to lead a session to provide a reflection upon lay vocation. I was ordained to the diaconate at St Mary's College and so am looking forward to saying Mass in the chapel again and seeing the place.

I came away with a long list of things to do. Vocations Day is several months away but it will soon arrive.

Mass offerings and intentions – *Wednesday 4th March*

There is a strong tradition amongst Catholics to arrange to have a Mass offered for a particular intention. Sometimes this can be for a person's health, the repose of someone's soul or often for a private intention. In my parish work I offer Mass for all sorts of people in all sorts of circumstances. It is usual for the person arranging for a Mass to be said to give the priest an offering.

Over the last three years I have offered masses in school at the request of students and never request an offering and I would refuse if anything was offered. However, there is something sacrificial about making an offering for a Mass which is important. I have therefore now developed a system whereby students offer their time and talents in exchange for a Mass being said for their intentions. I have produced cards which pupils must complete when they undertake acts of kindness, help in the library, clean the chapel, work on the fair-trade stall, altar serve, play music at Mass or do some other good work. When they have filled in a card then they can request that a Mass be said. This can also work retrospectively in some circumstances. It is proving fairly popular and at the moment every Mass has an intention linked to this new scheme.

Crowd control – *Friday 6th March*

During Mass today I had to ask a student to be quiet as he was messing about and trying to distract someone in front of him, disrupting others in the process. This always makes me cross as I should be able to concentrate on celebrating Mass and having to chastise pupils confuses my role.

The form tutor was very good and dealt with the situation afterwards. I find this really hard as I want students to feel comfortable and not be constrained by discipline but this needs to always be balanced with respecting the holiness of the Mass and the Blessed Sacrament. So many students do not have a sense of the sacred, even though they come from families that claim to be Catholic. It is the lack of respect for Jesus which upsets me the most. I try hard to make Mass a positive experience. We have lots of student involvement, an attractive chapel and lively and reflective music but still some choose to be disruptive and damage the atmosphere that we are trying to create. I always have to remind myself that the majority of students do respond positively and part of our vocation is to offer up these experiences to God.

I spent an hour in the Sixth Form LRC today and most of the time was taken up talking to a student who is thinking about studying theology at university. She has a real sense of vocation and God's purpose in her life but is not sure where or how this should be lived out. She feels that studying theology will give her the time to think about her relationship with God and what his plan for her life is. We talked about the colleges and universities that I knew about and different approaches to reading theology.

Flame 2 – *Saturday 7th March*

Today we took a group of students today to Flame 2 at Wembley Arena in London. This is a national youth event organised by the Catholic Youth Ministry Federation (CYMFED). We had been planning this for some time and were grateful that the Hinckley Circle of the Catenian Association had subsidised all of the students' entrance fees to the event, paying half of the total.

111

I find that the coach journey is often as important as the event itself. Like a medieval pilgrimage, it is a time to talk and get to know students a little bit more as we travel together. Flame 2 really was excellent. The day was filled with talks, worship, dance, music and drama. Cardinal Luis Tagle of Manilla spoke very powerfully and from the heart about Mercy. He was the speaker that the students seemed to respond to best. Other speakers included Timothy Radcliffe OP and Baroness Sheila Hollis. Timothy Radcliffe spoke of Adoration of the Blessed Sacrament not as 'Sun Bathing' but rather as 'Son Bathing'. This is something that I personally found helpful and I may develop this into a meditation for our time of Exposition in school.

For me the importance of these days is not necessarily the content but the fact that it gives young people the opportunity to see that there are other people of their own age in the Church. Often, even in Catholic schools, those pupils who are engaged in the faith are a minority. Spending today with several thousand other young people was a real celebration and statement that they are part of something bigger.

After reflecting upon today, I began to think that ten thousand is not that impressive a number. It is really only the equivalent of ten secondary schools. If all our schools and parishes supported such events and were full of staff and young people of faith, we could fill the whole of Hyde Park. These events are worthwhile but they are expensive and we must not allow ourselves to think that things are all well in the Church because we can fill Wembley Arena. There is a gap in our parishes where teenagers should be and our schools are not creating and fostering vocations in any significant numbers.

For the students that we took it was a day that they will remember and it certainly was a spirit-filled occasion.

3rd Week of Lent

Building the Kingdom – *Monday 9th March*

After the bell at 9am I led a singing practice for Year 7 during the assembly time. We learned some new music and also played a video clip of the song, 'Build your Kingdom', by Rend Collective. We also sang a new Lent song which has been used in some of our worship in the chapel. Keeping the singing going in a secondary school is always a challenge and these regular practices are essential. We try to make them fun and sing a mixture of new and familiar songs.

Dodgeball – *Wednesday 11th March*

Charities Afternoon occurs every year in Lent and students and staff plan and take part in various activities to raise money for the school charities. For the last couple of years, I have run a sponsored singalong at the local primary school which involved pupils getting sponsorship for leading an assembly and teaching the younger children some new songs. This is a popular event, but this year I wanted to take part in an event and support the Sixth Formers. So I put on my rarely used PE kit and joined the Sixth Form students who were running the Dodgeball event in the gymnasium. It was a really fun afternoon although I think I became a bit of a target and had to dodge the ball more than some of the others. It was interesting to think that I was dodging balls and running about today in the gym where usually I am at the altar saying Mass. How incarnational!

The Twelfth Station – *Friday 13th March*

The school chapel is too small to allow whole classes to go around the Stations of the Cross and so today I led a devotion based on the stations for a Year 9 group. This will happen with different groups over the next few weeks. We mostly used projected images but on occasions I made reference to the Stations of the Cross in the chapel, as we reflected upon the last few hours of Jesus' life.

The Stations of the Cross in the school chapel were made by pupils in pottery and are mounted on wooden backgrounds. They are low reliefs and some are a little too abstract for use in school. However, I always draw attention to the Twelfth Station, which is cracked and broken, and yet is still mounted on a board. The twelfth station of the cross focuses upon the crucifixion of Jesus. All of the other stations came out of the kiln intact but the Twelfth Station had shattered and this has since taken on a new significance and poignancy. I am so glad that they did not choose to fire another one. We reflected upon how Jesus' death had shattered death but also that His crucifixion was not the end of the story. From this shattered and broken station, when the curtain in the temple was torn in two, a new and brighter reality in the Resurrection dawns.

4th Week of Lent

Empowering priesthood – *Monday 16th March*

During Year 9 there is a focus within the RE curriculum on vocations, and students are taught a module on priesthood. Today I began a series of sessions where I reflected upon my own vocation. I have done this every year since I have been in school and enjoy the opportunity as it helps me to think more deeply about my own vocation. The students' questions also help me to focus upon what is important to me and assist my ongoing discernment.

As in the last few years, the questions today covered wide and varied aspects of priesthood, but a number of students asked me questions about married priests. I am a married priest and in most situations I see this as a strength. My vocation as a husband and father is very much interwoven into my calling to be a priest and the two complement each other in many ways. However, I am increasingly aware that in school I am modelling a form of vocation which none of the students can attain. Married priesthood is beyond their reach. One pupil today questioned why the Church allows me to be ordained but insists on celibacy in usual circumstances. I have to agree with him and it is a hard position to defend as it appears to be contradictory to insist on celibacy unless you were formerly an Anglican. I also cannot talk with any credibility about the challenges and joys of the celibate life. I will think about this further but I may try to get a celibate priest to come and talk next year, in addition to what I do during these sessions.

Planning the music – *Wednesday 18th March*

Today I met with students and staff to discuss the music that we may wish to introduce into the school liturgies over the next few months. We tend to introduce new music into the voluntary worship first and, if it works, we then have singing practice during the morning assemblies. There is so much good music being composed at the moment but we tend to focus on a few new pieces and try to do them well. It is always a challenge to have liturgically and seasonally appropriate music although we do aim to have music which reflects the main seasons of the Church year.

We have one or two really accomplished singers and musicians who are confident at leading any year group. They provide a fantastic role model for other students. During today's meeting we played through some of the chord sheets that I had printed off and one student simplified some of the music to make things more straightforward for playing in school. Although we have few musicians who play on a regular basis, this group are steadfast in their support. What they lack in numbers they certainly gain in enthusiasm and commitment. There are a number of musicians who will play occasionally but it is hard to convince them to be involved on a more regular basis.

Music is such a struggle in any secondary school. When I arrived, the liturgical music was jaded and few pupils played at all and so what we have now is a huge improvement. I am not really a musician and, whilst I do my best, I am constantly aware that the area of music is something that could be so much better than it is.

St Joseph plus one – *Friday 20th March*

Yesterday the Church celebrated the solemnity of St Joseph, husband of Mary and stepfather of Jesus. Before the 1970s the school was dedicated to St Joseph but when the community grew larger a new site was acquired and the dedication was changed.

We still have a large wooden low-relief carving at the back of the chapel by Carmel Cauchi as a reminder of our former patron. Today we remembered St Joseph at Mass. We reflected upon the fact that we know fairly little about St Joseph and that after Jesus' presentation in the Temple we don't hear any more about him. Often this is how the Christian life should be. We should be prepared to step out of the limelight and let Jesus be the one to shine out for all to see. It is about him and not us.

Later on this morning I led a further session on priesthood with students from Year 9. One student asked whether I had any inner conflicts. This was a really difficult question because the answer, if truthful, demonstrates the vulnerability which all Christians experience. I said that at times I feel hypocritical. I preach ideals which I myself don't always live up to. The difficulty of priesthood is that all of us are called to a ministry which we are not worthy of. We are all a works in progress and for clergy the proclamation of seemingly unobtainable truths is central to our vocation. We have to preach the ideal but we don't always practise what we preach because we are human. I hope that I answered honestly and clearly.

Mass today was offered for a student's mother who is pregnant.

5th Week of Lent

Sunday duty – *Sunday 22nd March*

On a usual Sunday I say Mass in my local parishes of English Martyrs, Hilmorton, and St Joseph's, Monks Kirby, near Rugby in Warwickshire. Occasionally I am asked to supply for priests who are away and today I said Mass in Our Lady of the Angels Church in Nuneaton. This is the church closest to the school and is a parish that I am familiar with. I like celebrating Mass in parishes within the catchment area of the school as it is an opportunity to see students in their home-parishes and also meet their parents. It is sadly noticeable how a large proportion of students in our Catholic schools are not part of the weekly worshipping community.

What astounds me more is how many students are practising Catholics and involved in serving, choirs, music groups and as readers and yet never get involved at school.

Today a student was the MC at the Mass and yet never comes near to the school chapel or volunteers to help in school liturgies. When I asked him why this was the case, he stated that he was worried about his friends' reaction if he were to serve in school. Before today I didn't know he was so involved in his parish.

It was a good morning and it is always useful to see how different parishes operate. I also chatted to a few parents at coffee after Mass. It proved to be a good occasion to build links and relationships.

More priesthood – *Monday 23rd March*

So often in school my time is taken up with resolving tensions that arise between students who fall out. Often they accuse each other of wrongdoing and forgiveness is something that we always end up working on. Today's Gospel reading deals powerfully with this thorny issue and reminds us of the healing nature of truly forgiving someone:

> Early in the morning he came again to the temple; all the people came to him, and he sat down and taught them. The scribes and the Pharisees brought a woman who had been caught in adultery, and placing her in the midst they said to him, 'Teacher, this woman has been caught in the act of adultery. Now in the law Moses commanded us to stone such. What do you say about her?' This they said to test him that they might have some charge to bring against him. Jesus bent down and wrote with his finger on the ground. And as they continued to ask him, he stood up and said to them, 'Let him who is without sin among you be the first to throw a stone at her.' And once more he bent down and wrote with his finger on the ground.

But when they heard it, they went away, one by one, beginning with the eldest, and Jesus was left alone with the woman standing before him. Jesus looked up and said to her, 'Woman, where are they? Has no one condemned you?' She said, 'No one, Lord.' And Jesus said, 'Neither do I condemn you; go, and do not sin again.' (John 8:2-11)

At Mass this morning there was a very long first reading from the Book of Daniel. I can see from their glazed appearances that this has no impact whatsoever on the students present and became background noise. The Gospel reading was the story of Jesus forgiving the woman who committed of adultery (John 8). Jesus tells those present that the one without sin should cast the first stone. At the conclusion of the story Jesus and the woman are left standing together alone. In the homily I reflected that this is how Jesus' forgiveness works. In the end we are on our own with Him and it is only to Him that we are ultimately answerable for all that we do.

Priesthood was the topic of the afternoon, as I spoke to another group as part of the series where I talk about my vocation. The questions were predictably similar to those that were asked on Friday. I talked about the roles a priest undertakes and those things that are important. On the whiteboard we constructed the diary of a typical week for a priest and then discussed what skills and qualities a priest needs to live out his calling. I became aware that in these sessions we only really thought about priesthood in terms of function. I did not successfully convey a more ontological view of priesthood and what it means to 'be' a priest. This is partly because these concepts are hard for Year 9 students to properly grasp; but I also feel that it may be a deeper issue of how we think about vocation in school and in the Church nowadays.

The day concluded with time spent in the Sixth Form LRC talking to students who were working on their A-level Art projects. Many of the projects seem to be quite dark and macabre and I wished that I had asked more about this at the time. I will have to try to catch them again and have a longer discussion.

General Election – *Wednesday 25th March* (*The Annunciation of the Lord*)

Over the last few weeks I have been leading services for each year group for the season of Lent. Today was the last one and each year group has had at least one service.

At Mass today we celebrated the feast of the Annunciation of Our Lord. This is when the Angel Gabriel visited Our Lady and asked her to conceive and give birth to Jesus. A good number of students were present today and one of the servers brought a group of his friends along who expressed a wish to train to be altar servers. During the homily we thought about the story of the Annunciation and reflected upon Our Lady's decision to say yes to God and the sacrifices and risks that she was taking. At the end of Mass, we turned and faced the statue of Our Lady in the rosary corner and sang a version of the *Magnificat* that we have been learning in school.

For several weeks I have been collecting newspaper articles, political leaflets and manifestos relating the general election taking place in May. Now that I have gathered together a good and balanced selection I presented them to the Sixth Form current affairs group. We spent the whole session looking at policies and thinking about the biases of the newspapers. It appears that the students are more right wing than I thought, especially when it comes to the welfare state. There was quite a lively debate, which is what I was hoping for.

The election seems far away but the coverage in the run-up is everywhere.

This is the last day that I will work with students in this term as Friday is a training day and then it is the Easter Holidays.

Safeguarding – *Friday 27th March*

The focus of the training day was safeguarding. This is now such an important part of working in a school and the training took nearly three hours. Mass was celebrated in the chapel at lunchtime and a good number of staff attended. During the homily we reflected upon a Catholic approach to supporting vulnerable students and I shared a little of my role. I very rarely talk about my work in this way and it is good for staff to have a clearer view of what I do so that they can feel confident to come to me for support.

It is good to finish today for the Easter holidays. For me things will remain busy for the next week as we enter Holy Week. I will celebrate the Triduum in my local parish before having a few days' break after Easter Sunday.

CHAPTER FIVE
Easter – May

2nd Week of Easter

He is risen. Alleluia! – *Monday 13th April*

We returned to school today after the Easter holiday but the season of Easter continues for a few more weeks yet. This morning I celebrated a Mass in the school hall for all the students in Year 7. Over the next two weeks every year group will have an Easter-themed celebration. There was a good serving team this morning and we filled the hall with the fragrance of incense. It was also lovely to hear the Easter songs that we have been practising sung with such gusto. Mass was offered for a staff member who is thinking about their future.

In place of the homily I had written something a little different. This really seemed to grab the attention of those present this morning. I started by giving a traditional homily about Easter and then, as planned, one student, who was playing in the band, threw his guitar down and stormed over to the sanctuary shouting that I was talking a load of rubbish. He brought the script alive beautifully. The room was silenced! He then talked about why he had a problem with the Resurrection and I answered his questions, which included: Wasn't it just a conspiracy? Surely Jesus wasn't really dead? Perhaps the disciples stole the body? It was early in the morning; maybe they got the wrong tomb? Did the Romans steal the body? Was he just in a coma and then revived?

I was really pleased with how this went and it was worth all the hard work and rehearsal time. Much of what we do in school involves so much preparation for something that only lasts for a short time.

This afternoon I met with a number of pupils in my office. I support a large number of pupils in this way at the moment. A chaplain is not the only worker within a Catholic school who has a role which is concerned with student welfare. In a modern secondary school it is common to have learning mentors, counsellors, family workers, pastoral tutors and heads of year who all have a concern for well-being. As a chaplain it is important to work with these other professionals for the good of the students we aim to help. Often staff can be guarded about their roles and resist partnership working but this is something that as chaplains we should seek to avoid. There have been times in the past when I have encountered major resistance from other professionals who wish to work alone. This can be dangerous. Some of the most high-profile child abuse cases in the last decade have been allowed to go unnoticed because professionals and different agencies have not communicated with each other. Chaplaincy is about building community and fostering unity. This vocation should be lived out in the way we work with others. Existing in our own furrows will not assist anyone.

An ordinary day – *Wednesday 15th April*

By school standards, today was fairly uneventful. My work was filled with the usual pattern of liturgies and meetings and most of the morning was spent in the library at the computer screen completing a risk assessment for a trip and producing posters for an event. I have also been asked to write some references for a couple of Sixth Form students who are applying for part-time jobs.

In contrast to my uneventful day our first reading at Mass today was full of drama:

> But the high priest rose up and all who were with him, that is, the party of the Sadducees, and filled with jealousy they arrested the apostles and put them in the common prison. But at night an angel of the Lord opened the prison doors and brought them out and said, 'Go and stand in the temple and speak to the people all the words of this Life.' And when they heard this, they entered the temple at daybreak and taught. Now the high priest came and those who were with him and called together the council and all the senate of Israel, and sent to the prison to have them brought. But when the officers came, they did not find them in the prison, and they returned and reported, 'We found the prison securely locked and the sentries standing at the doors, but when we opened it we found no one inside.' Now when the captain of the temple and the chief priests heard these words, they were much perplexed about them, wondering what this would come to. And someone came and told them, 'The men whom you put in prison are standing in the temple and teaching the people.' Then the captain with the officers went and brought them, but without violence, for they were afraid of being stoned by the people. (Acts 5:17-26)

Against the backdrop of this my day seems lacking in life. So much in ministry can seem mundane and routine. There is so much bureaucracy and administration which is unavoidable nowadays. Ministry in schools can be fun but this other aspect is also part of the reality.

I rarely work in the chaplaincy room and always try to base myself in the library as I feel that it makes me more available and easily accessible. Students and staff don't like to disturb me in the office but seem far more willing to just pop by and have a chat when I am in a more open area of the school. Aside from the playground I have most of my meaningful conversations with students and staff in the library. This makes working more difficult because I am constantly interrupted and things take twice as long, but the rewards outweigh the negatives.

At lunchtime we met in the chaplaincy room after Mass. It is far too small and many of the students who came to Mass could not get in. Things often get too loud and silly as the students are squeezed together tightly around the seating. It would be much better if we had a larger chaplaincy common room. Comfortably, the room seats about ten people, but today there must have been double that number. I have had to stop offering hot drinks as it is too dangerous, which is sad as this was part of my ministry of hospitality. Last week we tried to use a classroom but the students didn't like this. Most seem to appreciate the fact that there is a chaplaincy room set aside for the specific purposes of chaplaincy. I never refer to it as my office as I like it to be a place where students can feel a sense of ownership and belonging.

Running over – *Friday 17th April*

Our series of year-group masses for Easter continued today with a celebration for Year 10 students. We repeated our question-and-answer homily about Resurrection doubts. I have to be careful as we still have two more to do and I keep embellishing my lines so today it was a little too long. Keeping to time is important in school in order to retain students' attention, but more importantly to fit in with the timetable. So much of work in schools is determined by the bell and I am terrible at letting things run over into the next period. Most Friday masses run over and whilst pupils encourage me to take longer, it is not a responsible thing to do when time in school is so pressed and precious. There is always a balance to be struck. The liturgy should always take precedence in a Catholic school.

Today I started a new group for pupils who have experienced bereavement. I developed this in my first year in school when there were fourteen students who had lost a parent, sibling or close family member. Thankfully this year the group is a lot smaller. It is inexpressibly sad when students who are so young experience something so tragic as the loss of someone so close. This course is a very small way of helping them at this difficult time in their lives.

A chaplain has a unique role in supporting students before, during and after the losses that they can face. I have chosen to adopt a group work model following a set course that I have adapted slightly for our own needs. I continue to assist pupils on a one-to-one basis but group work is valuable as it introduces students to others in similar situations. Often things that are profoundly important are shared within the setting of the group and the participants start to support each other after the first few weeks.

3rd Week of Easter

Images of the Mass – *Monday 20th April*

At the Year 7 assembly today I led a meditation focusing on different images of the Mass. We started with prayers and the chapel musicians played a couple of songs. I then projected some images relating to aspects of the Mass onto the screen at the front of the hall.

The first image was a plug socket. This represented that when we celebrate Mass we enter into, or plug into, something that proceeds eternally. Mass is not just us celebrating in our own fallibility but rather we enter into worship that is much greater than ourselves and our own setting. All too often we only see the Mass in the here and now. The second image was a painting of heaven by Akaiane Kramarik, reminding us that the worship of heaven and the Mass are completely linked in a wonderful relationship.

Next we looked at familiar images of the Upper Room and thought about how through our celebration of the Mass we are invited into that room again with Jesus. We are present with him at the table following his commands to 'Do this in memory of me.'

Finally, I concluded with an image of the Mass at Calvary and shared what it means for the Mass to be a sacrifice. I also talked about masses being offered as a sacrifice for a particular intention and mentioned our Mass-intention scheme in school. It seemed to go down well and we concluded with a few more worship songs before the blessing.

The aim of the assembly was to help students begin to appreciate the great depth of the Mass as often many only view it in a very superficial way. Having a shallow understanding of the Mass, and faith in general, is often how boredom and indifference can set in. I am growing in my awareness that if we only give young people a superficial grasp of the sacred we can actually be inoculating them against the faith. In my role as a hospital chaplain I meet so many adults who do not practise any more. When I reflect with them why this is the case, it seems that they really only ever had a limited understanding. They seem to be stuck in a childish faith with a naive view of God, the Church and scripture. Many non-practising adults that I meet went to Catholic schools, were altar servers, attended Mass, belonged to youth groups but have left the Church. Good and engaging catechesis is essential. We cannot assume that the flame is passed on merely by osmosis, especially in today's context where the faith is infrequently taught and practised within Catholic families.

Cajon – *Wednesday 22nd April*

At this morning's Chaplaincy Council meeting we had a lively discussion about Year 7 students. Many of the older students feel irritated by the immaturity of some of the younger ones and they perceive that their behaviour is putting people off from coming to chaplaincy events. I explained that I remember most of them when they were in Year 7 and they were not that different. However, there is a serious point here and we discussed the possibility of having some age-specific groups and worship. I recognise that we need to be careful as too much division of the year groups could create exclusion. It is good for the younger ones to be alongside older and more responsible students. I agreed to investigate the possibilities of some activities just for older students beginning in the new school year in September.

Recently we received a donation towards the chapel from Mater Ecclesiae Convent and today we discussed ways in which this could be used. After suggestions ranging from the absurd to the bizarre we agreed to buy a Cajon with some of the money. This is a wooden box that acts as a drum kit. The drummer sits on top of the box and each side makes a different sound. We have a drummer who plays regularly for us but the drums are always too loud and we can never use them in chapel as the space is too small. A Cajon will be a great addition to our chapel instruments as we make a merry noise to the Lord. It is also much easier to play than a drum kit and so hopefully this can open up possibilities for a wider group of students.

Conversion – *Friday 24th April*

The first reading at Mass today was the account of the conversion of St Paul:

> But Saul, still breathing threats and murder against the disciples of the Lord, went to the high priest and asked him for letters to the synagogues at Damascus, so that if he found any belonging to the Way, men or women, he might bring them bound to Jerusalem. Now as he journeyed he approached Damascus, and suddenly a light from heaven flashed about him. And he fell to the ground and heard a voice saying to him, 'Saul, Saul, why do you persecute me?' And he said, 'Who are you, Lord?' And he said, 'I am Jesus, whom you are persecuting; but rise and enter the city, and you will be told what you are to do.' The men who were travelling with him stood speechless, hearing the voice but seeing no one. Saul arose from the ground; and when his eyes were opened, he could see nothing; so they led him by the hand and brought him into Damascus. And for three days he was without sight, and neither ate nor drank. Now there was a disciple at Damascus named Ananias. The

Lord said to him in a vision, 'Ananias.' And he said, 'Here I am, Lord.' And the Lord said to him, 'Rise and go to the street called Straight, and inquire in the house of Judas for a man of Tarsus named Saul; for behold, he is praying, and he has seen a man named Ananias come in and lay his hands on him so that he might regain his sight.' But Ananias answered, 'Lord, I have heard from many about this man, how much evil he has done to thy saints at Jerusalem; and here he has authority from the chief priests to bind all who call upon thy name.' But the Lord said to him, 'Go, for he is a chosen instrument of mine to carry my name before the Gentiles and kings and the sons of Israel; for I will show him how much he must suffer for the sake of my name.' So Ananias departed and entered the house. And laying his hands on him he said, 'Brother Saul, the Lord Jesus who appeared to you on the road by which you came, has sent me that you may regain your sight and be filled with the Holy Spirit.' And immediately something like scales fell from his eyes and he regained his sight. Then he rose and was baptized. (Acts 9:1-19)

In the homily I spoke about the life of Saul and how he had been transformed by an encounter with Jesus. We thought a little about Saul's 'CV' and how this made his conversion all the more dramatic and unexpected. Here was an educated and well-off man, a Roman citizen, business man and someone who today we may describe as a religious extremist. He would be the last person you would have expected to become a follower of Jesus. It was the encounter with Jesus that brought about his transformation and today lives can still be dramatically changed when we encounter the living Jesus.

I concluded with the reassurance that no matter how far away we may feel from God there is hope. Jesus is always there to greet us when we turn back to him. If we are open to His presence, we can be transformed into the people he is calling us to be. For Saul this meant having a complete watershed in life and having experiences that he never would have dreamed of in his old way of life. If he had reverted back to his old ways we would never have heard of him and he would have been lost in the obscurity of time. Today in this small insignificant chapel and throughout the world we listened to his life-changing encounter.

Sadly, when most of the students leave school this will often be the last time that they worship. Preaching the message that God will always be there for them and that the door is always open becomes increasingly important.

I am slowly appreciating these less dramatic days. All too often I feel that my ministry should be dramatic and busy but today has been a day for abiding. In school chaplaincy there is a tendency to always try to portray a Resurrection faith which is full of vitality, charisma and activity. I sometimes forget that in many ways the Resurrection was, at first, a low-key event that was witnessed only by a few of Jesus' closest friends. It was only after they had gathered together, hiding in the Upper Room, reflecting and praying that they gained the confidence and the strength to bring the Good News to bear in the world. The importance of the ordinary things is felt when Jesus shared breakfast with his friends shortly after his resurrection. This simple fellowship was what they needed after the trauma of Good Friday. We should not be afraid of the ordinary times for it is from these moments that the new life of Easter grows.

4th Week of Easter

Giving but not receiving – *Monday 27th April*

Mass this morning was offered for the husband of a member of staff who was unwell. I announced the Mass as a private intention as there were a number of students present and the member of staff may not have wanted everyone to know that he was unwell.

> 'Truly, truly, I say to you, he who does not enter the sheepfold by the door but climbs in by another way, that man is a thief and a robber; but he who enters by the door is the shepherd of the sheep. To him the gatekeeper opens; the sheep hear his voice, and he calls his own sheep by name and leads them out. When he has brought out all his own, he goes before them, and the sheep follow him, for they know his voice. A stranger they will not follow, but they will flee from him, for they do not know the voice of strangers.' This figure Jesus used with them, but they did not understand what he was saying to them. So Jesus again said to them, 'Truly, truly, I say to you, I am the door of the sheep. All who came before me are thieves and robbers; but the sheep did not heed them. I am the door; if any one enters by me, he will be saved, and will go in and out and find pasture. The thief comes only to steal and kill and destroy; I came that they may have life, and have it abundantly.' (John 10:1-10)

Many students that I come across are lost and do not know Jesus. They have encountered some of the thieves that Jesus describes. They don't seem to realise that the false shepherds of materialism, pornography, violence and the cult of celebrity will ultimately lead to a less meaningful life. So many people have swallowed the lies of the thieves who have deceived the sheep. We will only find life in its fullest abundance when we listen for the voice of the true shepherd. School chaplains have a huge responsibility to enable young people to hear this voice today.

I felt low today and have been working really hard lately. I am seeing a large number of pupils on a one-to-one basis as well as running groups and having a busy schedule in school. My work in the parish and the hospital is also hectic and I have had a couple of night-time calls during the weekend to the hospital.

School chaplaincy is often a thankless role. You can put so much energy into feeding and nurturing others and seem to get very little in return. There are times when I feel personally fed by my work but today I recognise that there is little mutuality in ministering to children and young people. In my parish work I get feedback and people ask after my well-being and family but in school there is little of this. I am supported by the RE department, but so much of a priest's role is working alone. This is equally so in the case of lay chaplains who work in our schools. Other clergy are around but also work in their own silos. There are times when I feel like a performer who always needs to be entertaining and in doing so I am not being spiritually fed myself. In my work in the parish, I feel a sense of spiritual communion with those I work alongside, but in school this does not always feel the case. Today I am glad that I am only part-time as my other work provides a much needed contrast. At times I contemplate requesting to become full-time but today I feel tired and can't wait for the end of the day to arrive.

Blessed are the peacemakers – *Wednesday 29th April (St Catherine of Siena)*

There were fewer at Mass today due to a house activity taking place at lunchtime. We gathered the benches around the altar and had a much more intimate celebration. Students read from their places and I sat in the circle with everyone else. Usually we celebrate Mass more formally, but occasionally it is good to have this level of informality, especially when numbers are down. It is unusual to have such small numbers and it takes me back to when I first introduced lunchtime Mass. For the first year it was a real struggle but things have developed well.

One of the biggest challenges today is the denial of sin. So many people don't recognise that their actions are sinful. My role as a confessor in school often involves guiding and advising students about what constitutes a sin and how to deal with it so as not to allow sins to become a burden or something destructive. I once helped out hearing confessions in a school where the RE coordinator did not like to use the term sin. All sorts of evasive phrases were used to explain the times when we make the wrong choices but the 'S'-word was not to be mentioned. I was reminded of this in the first reading today:

> This is the message we have heard from him and proclaim to you, that God is light and in him is no darkness at all. If we say we have fellowship with him while we walk in darkness, we lie and do not live according to the truth; but if we walk in the light, as he is in the light, we have fellowship with one another, and the blood of Jesus his Son cleanses us from all sin. If we say we have no sin, we deceive ourselves, and the truth is not in us. If we confess our sins, he is faithful and just, and will forgive our sins and cleanse us from all unrighteousness. If we say we

have not sinned, we make him a liar, and his word is not in us. My little children, I am writing this to you so that you may not sin; but if any one does sin, we have an advocate with the Father, Jesus Christ the righteous; and he is the expiation for our sins, and not for ours only but also for the sins of the whole world. (1 John 1:5 – 2:2)

Students regularly seek my help when disputes occur between them. After lunchtime today, a delegation was waiting in the chaplaincy room to tell me about two students who had fallen out, and as a consequence two groups of friends were now on bad terms with each other. This is often very trivial and can be dealt with easily but such things can get out of hand if not dealt with as soon as they arise. I sent most of the students away and the two who had fallen out remained with me. We talked about what had happened and then at the end they seemed to make things good. I advised them to keep a distance from each other for a while and agreed to see them both separately in a few days' time. By then I imagine it will all be forgotten. We prayed for forgiveness and healing.

Often I have to deal with things that seem trivial to an adult's understanding. Listening to teenage angst is very central to what I do. I am always careful to be seen to treat things seriously and not play them down. Sometimes this is hard and I feel like telling students to get a grip, but this would be self-defeating and they would no longer confide and trust in me.

5th Week of Easter

May Day – *Monday 4th May*
(The Forty Martyrs of England and Wales)

Today was a Bank Holiday and it was a real relief this morning not to have to get up in time for the early morning Mass. School is open again tomorrow. I said a Mass this evening for the sisters at Mater Ecclesiae. The day was spent on a family bike ride.

Boundaries – *Wednesday 6th May*

Boundaries are important in schools and are essential in all work with young people and children. In my role, students do view me differently from other members of staff, which can result in some inappropriate behaviour at times. Today a pupil put his arm around me in what was a friendly gesture. I am aware as a priest that I have to be really careful in the way I conduct myself with students, especially bearing in mind some of the recent history in the Catholic Church. There have been many times when students have tried to be affectionate towards me, but I always have to explain that this cannot happen and that it isn't appropriate.

In many ways this is really sad but in the present climate staff have to be so careful and vigilant. Physical contact can seem such a natural human expression but any physical contact can be misinterpreted. Students do feel affection towards staff and we naturally develop positive and friendly relationships with some students, but we always need to remember that we are in professional roles. Safeguarding is so important and as a school we have such a duty of care to ensure the safety and well-being of those in our care.

Today I just explained very carefully to the student that he shouldn't put his arm around staff and said that we can show our appreciation and affection in other ways.

Queen of the May – *Friday 8th May*

Today one of the RE department arranged with me to have a May Devotion for her class. I exposed the Blessed Sacrament upon the altar and then she and some of her class led the rosary. Using the chapel within the timetable more is something that I would like to develop further and I feel I may offer this to some of the other teachers in the future.

The American author Fredrica Mathewes-Green describes her local church as an 'Outpost of Eternity'. For me this is a really important concept. I often speak about the chapel in this way. Even though our school chapel is only a converted classroom, Jesus is present in the tabernacle and it is a place of peace in a bustling and crowded school. Today I caught a group of pupils who were messing about in the chapel again. It was only low-level poor behaviour but it prevents others from using the chapel for its proper purpose. I had to speak to them and then lock the door for a few hours. I never shout at students, but I do challenge them when they fall short of the expectations that we as a school have for them. I seem to be constantly claiming the chapel as a sacred place. Here we meet Jesus, and in his presence he would want us to be ourselves, but it is also important that students learn propriety and respect. This is an ongoing process of calling students to greater holiness, giving them the space and opportunity to encounter Jesus.

Today's Mass was offered for a parent with cancer.

6th Week of Easter

A parallel liturgical universe – *Wednesday 13th May*

There are times when I feel that I am guilty of creating what I term 'A Parallel Liturgical Reality'. By this I mean that I create a style of worship which aims to be engaging and lively but which cannot really be found in many normal parishes in the real world. It is my desire to help students know Jesus' love through a liturgy that means something to them and speaks to their hearts. Whilst being a stickler for the *General Instruction of the Roman Missal*, which directs how Mass should be celebrated, I am willing to be experimental in terms of music and non-Eucharistic worship. In school, most masses will have a full serving team in order to allow fuller participation of students and there are always lively worship songs and Mass settings. Homilies in the chapel are nearly always interactive and are more like a conversation or group discussion than a traditional sermon. My aim is that students feel free to express themselves in worship and some do get a little carried away at times. I believe this is a good thing, but it does have a more negative side and this was brought home to me by a conversation that I had with a pupil that I shall call 'Will'.

Will is a Catholic who has never really practised his faith. He was baptised as a baby but the family rarely went to Mass during his childhood. He made his First Communion and confession in Year 3 and then was confirmed when in Year 6. He is now in Year 11 and has been coming to Mass and other worship on a voluntary basis for the last two years. At the weekend he decided that he would like to go to a Sunday Mass in his local parish and persuaded his reluctant grandmother to go with him. He found it lacking and came to speak to me about it. He reported that the music was dull, nobody sang and at the end people were leaving before the final hymn had finished. This has led him to perceive that the people present lacked commitment to their faith. He recognised the Mass but everything else was unfamiliar to him. Will also noted that there were only a very few people of his own age at the Mass.

This conversation, which is not the first of this kind, does make me question whether I have chosen the right approach. Am I giving the young people in my school the wrong image of the Catholic faith? Am I setting them up for a fall? How can we bridge the gap between the worship at school and the reality of parish life?

Rosary Relay – *Friday 15th May*
(Friday before the Ascension)

We took part in a Rosary Relay today. After Mass we set up the chapel for rosary and Exposition of the Blessed Sacrament and waited for Our Lady to arrive. A statue was handed on from school to school and at each stop an act of worship took place. Six schools took place in this special event. St Anne's Primary School delivered the statue to us and we had to pass it on to St Francis' School, which was the next link in the chain. About fifty students took part in the worship in our school and then a small group of students accompanied me to pass on the prayers. The Rosary Club led the prayers, and the musicians some songs at the end. This was a good way of bringing all our schools together in prayer, especially as we now form the Holy Spirit Academy and are seeking to work much more closely with each other.

We offered Mass for a student who has a trial for the RAF at the weekend. He hopes to enter next year.

7th Week of Easter

Christ the healer – *Wednesday 20th May*

This lunchtime after Mass I arranged to see two students who had asked to make their confession. This happens fairly often now and a number of students have got into a pattern of regularly availing themselves of the sacrament. I always value such requests as it demonstrates that a student has made an effort and commitment to take the sacrament and their spiritual life seriously. If I am being honest, it also makes me feel useful and wanted.

There is a reasonably good uptake of confession in school at the moment, on both these individually arranged occasions as well as during timetabled sessions. Catholic schools have an important and prophetic role to play in the wider work of reconciliation and wholeness which is rooted in the Gospel of divine forgiveness. Sadly, this is often underdeveloped in many of the schools that I know. This is partly due to a limited number of clergy. If all the students in a secondary school wanted to make their confession, a whole deanery of clergy would be needed.

As a priest I am aware that I am only one among many professionals and agencies who work with students in a welfare and well-being capacity. Teachers, school nurses, social workers, mental health professionals and youth workers all have a significant and valuable input into the troubles and struggles of many of the students that I support. Catholic schools, and chaplaincy in particular, have something significant to offer in the lives of students alongside other forms of social and medical intervention.

The recognition of sin and forgiveness in the context of God's ever-abundant grace should be a central part of a school and chaplain's proclamation and ministry. This has a wonderful capacity to bring healing. Most forms of therapeutic work require a level of self-awareness in order to be effective. Growing into the sacrament of reconciliation can be a journey of discovery of the self in relation to God. Examination of conscience with the assurance of the forgiveness of sins is incredibly therapeutic and offers something which is found in no other professional discipline. This is a unique gift that we have to offer.

All of a school chaplain's work including one-to-one pastoral support, the celebration of the sacraments, preaching, teaching and prayer, is rooted in the Good News of God's reconciling love. Only this love can completely repair brokenness and bring healing and oneness to students' situations. Placed alongside and in partnership with secular interventions this can be something really powerful.

I never view my role as being in competition with other agencies and workers at all. I would always encourage students to seek outside help and support when necessary. My background as a social worker means that such interdisciplinary working is part of my DNA and I regularly work with other professionals in supporting students. Chaplaincy opens up a further dimension for the healing of the whole person in the context of the divine.

Sixth Form Leavers' Mass – *Thursday 21st May*

This afternoon I celebrated the Sixth Form Leavers' Mass. There was good participation from both staff and students. I found it encouraging that a number of parents had responded positively to the invitation to attend. I offered the Mass for all present, for their exams and for their future hopes and aspirations. It is always an emotional occasion and for most of the students this finally ends a seven-year relationship with this school and fourteen years in Catholic education. Non-Catholic pupils and staff also seemed to respond well and I was overwhelmed that all the staff who were not Catholic came forward for a blessing. It must be difficult for them, and yet today they showed their support in a simple and public way.

Leavers' Mass (another one) – *Friday 22nd May*

This afternoon we celebrated Mass in the hall for all the students in Year 11 who are leaving. After today they go on exam-leave and finally finish in about one month's time. The last day has become a real rite of passage and is filled with lots of goodbyes and an opportunity to sign the many leavers' books and to feature in the ubiquitous 'selfies'.

For a number of the students it will not be a complete goodbye as they will go on to the Sixth Form in September, but many are leaving to go on to vocational courses, apprenticeships and other colleges.

At the beginning of Mass I had to ask the students to be respectful as the first hymn was a little raucous and was not very dignified. The excitement of the day always makes celebrations like this a little lively. So we had a few moments silence to collect our thoughts and the rest of the Mass was a happy and reverent occasion. The music and singing was excellent and the band really pulled out all of the stops to make this a celebration. The last hymn, 'Sing it in the Valleys', has become a sort of the school hymn and was sang with such gusto. I really can't stand this hymn but it is so embedded in the life of the school that nearly all major celebrations end with it. Last year I omitted it from the Sixth Form Leavers' Mass and students were upset that we missed it. So 'Sing it in the Valleys' is one of the crosses that I will have to bear for the rest of my ministry in school.

For many students this will sadly be their last time of worship for a long time. Many do not go to Mass in their local church and I just hope and pray that during these last few years some seeds may have been sown that will bear fruit in the future. It was also sad to say goodbye to three of the altar servers. They have been so faithful and supportive and I was glad that they were so enthusiastic to serve at their own Leavers' Mass. The thurifer ensured that the whole place was in a cloud of smoke. I recalled that one of the altar servers had once said he measured his success by the amount of coughs he induced!

CHAPTER SIX
Summer Term

9th Week in Ordinary Time

Franciscan Sisters of the Renewal – *Monday 1st June (St Justin Martyr)*

The readings set for Mass really spoke into all that went on today. I very rarely alter the readings that are set and very often I find that they can provide just what is necessary and today's reading (Matthew 5:13-19) was no exception,

> You are the salt of the earth; but if salt has lost its taste, how shall its saltiness be restored? It is no longer good for anything except to be thrown out and trodden under foot by men. You are the light of the world. A city set on a hill cannot be hid. Nor do men light a lamp and put it under a bushel, but on a stand, and it gives light to all in the house. Let your light so shine before men, that they may see your good works and give glory to your Father who is in heaven. (Matthew 5:13-16).

Our visitors for the day were Sister Jacinta and Sister Josephine of the Franciscan Sisters of the Renewal. They came to lead a day of reflection and teaching about Jesus' presence in the Blessed Sacrament. They certainly did not keep their light hidden and it was an awe-inspiring day. The sisters are fantastic witnesses of Christ and shared their faith beautifully with the students in a very simple and direct way. Many students fed back about the great feeling of peace that they felt whilst praying with the sisters in the presence of Jesus contained in the Blessed Sacrament.

The Franciscan Sisters of the Renewal were founded in 1988 in the Bronx area of New York. The aim of the Community is to live out Gospel values in simplicity according to the ideals of St Francis. They live in poor communities and if it becomes a community becomes wealthier they move on. The spiritual values uniting the sisters are personal and communal commitment to Jesus Christ. Adoration of the Blessed Sacrament is central to the sisters' life and mission.

The sisters ran five hour-long workshops with about fifty students in each group. They spoke for the first half of each session about their personal relationship with Jesus and Sister Josephine taught the students some new worship songs. You could tell that they spoke from a place of deep personal encounter with Jesus. Jesus wasn't some distant person to them but someone who was at the very centre of their being. Sister Jacinta addressed the students in her American drawl about 'dissing' Jesus when we do not genuflect to the Blessed Sacrament in the tabernacle. For several weeks afterwards this saying stuck with the students. When someone forgot to genuflect another student always shouted out, 'Don't diss.' The sisters' powerful yet gentle proclamation spoke of their radical lifestyle and deep love of Jesus, who is at the centre of their lives. This is something that I feel I struggle to convey in my own ministry. I have a deep love of Jesus but sometimes feel that I hide it too well. In the second half of each session, I exposed the

Blessed Sacrament upon the altar and then the sisters led devotions. We have Exposition in school several times each week and often as part of an RE lesson, but this experience spoke powerfully to those staff and students present, who were visibly moved by the experience.

Sister Jacinta spoke of Adoration a great deal. In school I have tended to just refer to praying before the Blessed Sacrament as Exposition, but following today I feel I will change this and develop a new approach. Using the term Adoration expresses clearly that the focus is on Jesus and not us. In school I am often tempted to make worship entertaining but all that we do should be for an audience of one. To adore is to be drawn away from our own busyness and self-centredness and be led in to the presence of Jesus and his love. In a school which is so busy and preoccupied this is all the more crucial.

Let them eat cake – *Wednesday 3rd June*
(St Charles Lwanga and the Martyrs of Uganda)

Today, after Mass, one of the altar servers brought a cake that he had baked at home. He explained that it was a rosary cake. On the top of the circular cake there was a rosary made out of icing and chocolate buttons and around the side the mysteries of the rosary were written. He is one of the most committed students and this was a lovely gesture. He said that he had also made one for the Rosary Club. So, as I cut the cake, we said the Hail Mary prayer and then enjoyed the creation.

The students talked about this week's visit from the Franciscan Sisters of the Renewal. They really seemed to have caught their imagination. I was asked whether we could arrange a trip to the Bronx to see the sisters but I explained that these particular sisters lived in Leeds which had less of an appeal.

The deacon – *Friday 5th June*
(St Boniface)

It was good to have a deacon at Mass this morning. Ray is visiting, as he is discerning whether school chaplaincy may be a form of ministry that he wishes to pursue in the future as part of his vocation. He is involved in his parish but would like to have something which could lead him away from his secular work. If Catholic education is to be sustained, then we need to encourage vocations to all aspects of school life. I regularly invite people into school to have a look around and remind Catholic teachers who work in non-Catholic schools that we need them!

We spent the morning looking around the school and chatting to different groups in the Sixth Form. At break time we visited the staff room. Having Ray with me made me realise how daunting a secondary school staff room can be for the first time. I remember my first visit to my local school when I was first ordained. Nobody spoke to me and the staff were all chatting away in their own departments. I didn't understand the culture or the language of schools then, and everything seemed so alien. I remember that I could not wait to get out of the place. When all the staff are together at St Thomas More I can imagine how enormous it all seems. Students are always knocking at the door wanting to see staff for things that are apparently too urgent to wait. With only a fifteen-minute break it is a fraught time in which to get a drink, speak to colleagues, check your pigeonhole, make a phone call, and so, for a visitor, it can be an unusual experience. Greeting clerical visitors may also not be that much of a priority to the busy staff. I introduced Ray to a few people before the bell went. We always live by the bell.

Mass this morning was offered for the repose of the soul of a grandfather.

10th Week in Ordinary Time

Into His presence – *Monday 8th June*

Adoration was much more formal today as the altar servers had asked whether they could be involved and use incense. I have grown in appreciation of these times of prayer and am less anxious now that the students are so used to praying in silence. Before, I always felt that I had to monitor behaviour and move things on when students became restless, but now I can relax more.

On these occasions I am always taken with the noise outside. The buzz of the playground filters through the windows at the back of the chapel. This reminds me of our role in praying for the whole community. Those outside may be indifferent to what goes on during these lunchtime services but we always keep them at the forefront of what we are offering to God. Aaron, Israel's High Priest, used to enter the Holy of Holies with jewels on his breastplate representing the twelve tribes of Israel. He was their priest and he went into God's presence with his people near to his heart.

> And you shall take two onyx stones, and engrave on them the names of the sons of Israel, six of their names on the one stone, and the names of the remaining six on the other stone, in the order of their birth. As a jeweller engraves signets, so shall you engrave the two stones with the names of the sons of Israel; you shall enclose them in settings of gold filigree. And you shall set the two stones upon the shoulder-pieces of the ephod, as stones of remembrance for the sons of Israel; and Aaron shall bear their names before the Lord upon his two shoulders for remembrance. (Exodus 28:9-12)

I feel this very keenly when I pray in Jesus' presence in the Blessed Sacrament and when I celebrate Mass in school. I carry the students and staff in my heart as I encounter God's living presence. This can mean bearing their joys, frustrations, foibles, and needs. Part of a school chaplain's role is to be with God for the whole community. Those who attend chapel are beginning to share in this vocation and this is reflected in the prayers that they say aloud, which always include prayers for situations and individuals in school.

Recollection – *Wednesday 10th June*

We set off in the minibus early this morning to Mater Ecclesiae for the Chaplaincy Council and Servers Recollection Day. I have arranged this day annually for the last few years partly as a thank you to those who help in the chaplaincy. The main aim of the day is to enable us gather together to pray and reflect about our work.

We started the day in the convent chapel with Morning Prayer led by two of the students. After tea and coffee, I gave everyone a piece of paper and told them all to go off into the grounds on their own and write or draw something about their good and more challenging experiences of being involved in the chaplaincy. It was really interesting to note that they couldn't cope with being alone. As I walked around to keep an eye on things, I noticed that they had naturally clustered together in groups and my attempts to separate them were in vain.

After a plenary on this exercise, we had a game of football on the front lawn and then celebrated Mass, together with the sisters, before having a picnic in the gardens. I love these days and especially the way the secular and the sacred are blended. It is important to have fun activities as part of the day and today it certainly added to the feeling of celebration.

The afternoon session started with a meditation based on an experience that moved me several years ago. Aware that young people, and especially Catholics, often face much peer pressure, I thought reflecting upon this story would help them.

When I was at college, my tutor organised a day retreat. Early in the morning, we set off in the minibus for a day of prayer, worship, reflection and praise. I was well used to going on retreats and pictured a beautiful retreat house in the country where the food was wholesome and the views splendid, or a serene convent where the sisters were kindly and prayerful. As we got closer to the retreat location, I realised that this would be like no other quiet day I had ever been on before. We entered a tough housing estate which clearly had experienced much deprivation and many social problems. The shops were boarded up and we passed a car that had been abandoned and then burnt out. I wondered where on earth my college tutor was taking us. As we arrived at the top of a hill we saw before us the Church of the Holy Cross. It was very unprepossessing with large metal fences topped with barbed wire surrounding the site. The church was a large concrete box with tiny windows which were barred for security. Inside the church, the atmosphere was more tranquil and we sat and listened to the talks, reflections and worshipped together. During the day I noticed a pile of rubble underneath the altar. Why was this collection of bricks, concrete, metal, wood and glass placed in such a prominent place? I became distracted by this and kept looking all day at that pile. At the end I asked the priest why it was there. He explained that every time a rock, piece of rubble or brick was thrown through a church window or at a car or even at a parishioner, they placed the item under the altar and prayed for the person who threw it. Every time the community worshiped, that was their focus. Praying for their persecutors as they gathered around God's table and offering it up with the Mass had become their charism.

Praying for our persecutors is hard, especially for these young people. Already they have the wisdom to offer it up and to carry on serving God in their school and parishes. We ended the day with a final game of football and headed back to school.

Sweet Heart of Jesus – *Friday 12th June*
(Sacred Heart of Jesus)

We celebrated the solemnity of the Sacred Heart today with a class of Year 8 students and a good number of volunteers present. During the homily I shared that the word courage has as its root the Latin word 'cor' which means heart. When we think of the Sacred Heart we traditionally reflect on Jesus' divine love and today we thought about how courage forms part of the deep love of Jesus.

I asked those present about ways in which we can courageously share Jesus' love with others in school. One of the servers said that serving needed courage as you had to not mind what people may think of you. One of the form-group members said that not joining in when others were being teased needed courage. This is certainly an important message for young people. Often it is easy to go along with the crowd and bow to pressure. I concluded with the words of John F Kennedy, himself paraphrasing Edmund Burke, 'For evil men to accomplish their purpose it is only necessary that good men should do nothing.'

Our young people can become extensions of Jesus' divine love but they need to find the courage to stand up and be real men and women. Surely this enablement should be at the heart of what a Catholic school seeks to do. Schools are called to be centres of formation in God's love. This love is tough and not sentimental. It can also be life changing if we allow ourselves to be transformed by it.

I spent some time in the Sixth Form LRC this morning. It is fairly quiet as students in Year 13 are currently doing exams and have completed their programme of teaching. One of the chapel guitarists was there and we had a chat about music and how to encourage some of the younger musicians, especially as he will be leaving to hopefully go to university next year.

11th Week in Ordinary Time

Fostering vocations – *Monday 15th June*

After Mass this morning, which was offered for a member of staff's husband, I visited all the Year 9 form-groups to try to encourage them to sign up for Vocations Day. At present the uptake has been poor and we have booked coaches and spent a great deal of time planning the event. I really did a hard sell. I cannot believe the apparent lack of interest. When I was at school I would have taken every opportunity to get out of school. By the end, a few more had signed up and I am confident that when things start to roll and the word gets around we will fill the coaches. Students are hesitant as they wish to know whether their friendship groups are going.

I spent this afternoon with a group of art students in the Sixth Form who told me about their projects. Their work is really impressive and it is good to see the talent and passion that these students have.

Sister act – *Wednesday 17th June*

During Mass today we thought about our own integrity as Christians and the need for our outward appearance to match our inner reality. In today's Gospel reading Jesus makes this quite clear,

> Beware of practising your piety before men in order to be seen by them; for then you will have no reward from your Father who is in heaven. Thus, when you give alms, sound no trumpet before you, as the hypocrites do in the synagogues and in the streets, that they may be praised by men. Truly, I say to you, they have their reward. But when you give alms, do not let your left hand know what your right hand is doing, so that your alms may be in secret; and your Father who sees in secret will reward you. And when you pray, you must not be like the hypocrites; for they love to stand and pray in the synagogues and at the street corners, that they may be seen by men. Truly, I say to you, they have their reward. But when you pray, go into your room and shut the door and pray to your Father who is in secret; and your Father who sees in secret will reward you... And when you fast, do not look dismal, like the hypocrites, for they disfigure their faces that their fasting may be seen by men. Truly, I say to you, they have their reward. But when you fast, anoint your head and wash your face, that your fasting may not be seen by men but by your Father who is in secret; and your Father who sees in secret will reward you. (Matthew 6:1-6. 16-18)

I concluded by making the point that Jesus isn't saying that outward things don't matter but rather that these things should be done simply and for God's glory alone.

Sister Maria spent the day in school today. She has just entered the noviciate at Mater Ecclesiae Convent and is exploring different forms of ministry that she may wish to pursue as part of her formation. Mater Ecclesiae is a semi-contemplative community and outside work is important. Sister Maria is interested in developing work with young people. Normally novices are not called 'Sister' but we thought that it would be easier in school to use the title.

If Sister Maria enjoys school work it is my hope that she may develop a ministry with some of the girls in school. Much of my work is with boys in school and most of those who attend chapel or come to chaplaincy events are male and so it will be good to have someone who can balance things up a little. Sister Maria spent the day shadowing me and spoke to the children after the lunchtime Mass. She will come in once each week until the end of term to get a feel for the place and see if things are for her.

This afternoon was sports day which is held on the playing field. I had a walk around and talked to some of those taking part and the staff who were supervising the events. As chaplains we can feel guilty when outwardly we appear to not be doing much but this ministry of availability is vitally important and yet so undervalued.

The sparkler – *Friday 19th June*

A good day. Mass was celebrated with a Year 7 form group today and there were a good number of volunteers present as well as some staff who were free and decided to come along.

I used one of my favourite homily props today as it fitted well with the Gospel reading,

> Do not lay up for yourselves treasures on earth, where
> moth and rust consume and where thieves break

in and steal, but lay up for yourselves treasures in heaven, where neither moth nor rust consumes and where thieves do not break in and steal. For where your treasure is, there will your heart be also. The eye is the lamp of the body. So, if your eye is sound, your whole body will be full of light; but if your eye is not sound, your whole body will be full of darkness. If then the light in you is darkness, how great is the darkness! (Matthew 6:19-23)

I don't usually use props in secondary school but today I lit a sparkler at the end of the Gospel and asked the students to describe the flame. They described it as being hot in the middle, shooting out, flying everywhere, as well as lots of other descriptions. I then said that this is how our faith should be. We need to be people who are full of light. Our hearts should burn from within for love of Jesus and this intensity should influence our whole lives and shine out for all to see. We should be like that sparkler as people who are transformed into living flames by the deep love of Jesus within.

I use lots of visual aids in my work in primary schools and have created myself some angst with this recently. I feel a real pressure to come up with something new and different. I have used Jenga, balloons, magic tricks, and even a bow and arrow. Many Wednesday nights and Thursday mornings have been spent rifling through my garage and cupboards to find the latest prop. At times I have a great prop but just can't think of any way of linking it to the Gospel of the day. This has created an expectation. Recently, when greeting the children at the door of the church, one child asked me what I had got in my bag today. They now expect something exciting every week. I have to be careful not to become a bit of a low-grade children's entertainer. These things can detract from the power of the Gospel.

12th Week in Ordinary Time

House prayer – *Monday 22nd June*
(Ss John Fisher and Thomas More)

A member of staff who has just taken on the responsibility of head of house asked me today if I could write her a prayer for when the house has assemblies. The house is named after St Ralph Sherwin, one of the forty martyrs of England and Wales. St Ralph was born in Derbyshire and educated at Eton College and then Exeter College, Oxford. He travelled to Rome where he trained for the priesthood. After his ordination he was arrested in London and is later renowned for converting fellow inmates whilst in prison. He was executed at Tyburn in 1581, his last words were, 'Jesu, Jesu, Jesu, esto mihi Jesus!' (Jesus, Jesus, Jesus, be to me a Jesus).

I wrote several prayers and also sent a few collects and some other prayers which I thought may be appropriate. I was pleased that a member of staff had thought of this. A number of Catholic schools have houses named after saints and often they can seem to become detached from their patron saint. It was good that this member of staff was making this a focus.

Today was the school feast day, although we have transferred this to later in the week.

The forerunner – *Wednesday 24th June*
(St John the Baptist)

During the lunchtime Mass we celebrated the solemnity of the Birth of St John the Baptist. I explained a little about St

John's role as a forerunner to Jesus. I then asked the students to suggest ways in which they could be forerunners to Jesus. They spoke of telling others about him, not taking the limelight when altar serving or playing music, inviting others to the chapel and being kind and compassionate in the role of a prefect. The list went on.

I grew up in a parish dedicated to St John the Baptist and have always had a devotion to him. His life provides a pattern for all Christian vocation. A true vocation is one which allows people to see Jesus for themselves. We are only enablers and supporters on the journey.

This afternoon I was asked to visit one of the deputy head teachers. During the meeting she asked whether I would consider doing some teaching next year. This would involve working additional hours and teaching some RE lessons. I was a little taken aback and said that I would have a think about it and let her know.

I am anxious about teaching. This is not because I feel that I couldn't do the role but because I perceive that it could impact upon my relationship with the students. There is a long history of chaplains also teaching. Many independent schools continue with this pattern today but I like the fact that my role is purely pastoral and liturgical. Would students come to me for help still if I had recently placed them in detention? The relationship that I have is completely different from that of a teacher. Students do have positive relationships with teachers and so it is possible for a balance to be struck, but I would not want to jeopardise what I have established. In addition, I am not a qualified teacher and when I was a social worker I always had issues with unqualified workers who took on much of the qualified workers' roles. At the time I perceived their presence as something which undermined the social work profession. I wouldn't want to be in a position where I felt I was doing a similar thing to my colleagues and friends in school. Teaching is a very particular vocation and whilst I feel that part of my vocation is to work with young people, I am not sure that I am called to be a school teacher. I will have to think and pray about this a lot more before giving any response.

St Thomas More, pray for us – *Friday 26th June* *(St Thomas More – transferred)*

We usually transfer the memorial of St Thomas More, our feast of title, to a nearby Friday and this afternoon, following all the usual preparations, we celebrated Mass as whole school in the gymnasium. I arrived at the altar feeling frazzled. Some of the younger altar servers get a little excited and the older ones don't always help in calming them down. Ten minutes before the Mass all the albs got mixed up and we still had to make our way over to the gym to light all the candles and get the thurible lit and incense going. This sort of thing always happens and I was glad when a member of staff came to act as MC. He is an altar server in his own parish and it is great that he can take care of things during the ass.

The students don't normally need an adult with them but at whole school masses it gives me some reassurance and also helps if something goes wrong. Today I smashed the glass picture frame containing the image of St Thomas More. This was propped up in a stand in front of the altar and I knocked it over when I censed the altar at the beginning of Mass. There was glass all over the floor and the picture had fallen from the staging which formed the sanctuary and there was a mighty crash. Having another adult with me at the front was a real asset, as the other servers would not have dealt with it as discreetly as he did. I'm not sure this is the way in which I had intended to honour St Thomas More on his special day.

When I felt that one of the hymns had not been sung that well, I started singing it again acapella from the altar and slowly everyone joined in. By the end we raised the roof and the sound of hundreds of teenagers' voices echoing around the room was haunting and beautiful. After Communion, a student sang a solo of 'Pie Jesu' by Andrew Lloyd Webber. The whole place was stunned by her elegant voice and her bravery at stepping out from the crowd. Peer pressure and the worry of what other students will say often prevent even the most talented students from getting involved. I am always saddened by how many grade 8 musicians and competent readers will not get involved because they worry what others will think. During the thank-yous after Mass she had a huge round of applause.

It is always difficult to create a sense of the sacred in a secular place like a gym. There are many factors to consider. Student behaviour has to be monitored in such a large-scale environment and there is always a potential for even the smallest incident to escalate into something much larger. In my time I have not noticed any major problems and behaviour and participation is generally good. Staff are conscientious but it does mean that they cannot enter into worship fully as they always have to keep one eye on their class. The larger celebration naturally takes on a less intimate and more formal feel and this is something that I personally struggle with.

Mass was offered for the aunt of a staff member who had recently died.

13th Week in Ordinary Time

Vocations Day – *Monday 29th June*
(Ss Peter and Paul was transferred to the Sunday this year)

Today just over one hundred pupils and staff boarded the coaches for St Mary's College, Oscott. After all the cajoling and chasing up over the last few weeks I was pleased with the number of students who attended. All the staff agreed that this was the right number and we were glad there were no more students as the accommodation at Oscott, especially at lunchtime, was a little tightly stretched.

Oscott is a really dramatic place to hold our vocations conference and the buildings, to a large extent, speak for themselves. The Gothic grandeur is largely thanks to the architect Joseph Potter and there are many fittings and furnishings by Pugin. The pupils were awestruck as we stepped from the coaches onto the front lawn. One student shouted out that it was like Hogwarts School.

The day was led by the seminarians, Chris, David, Pascal, Matt and Kevin, who were the most wonderful facilitators and were very attentive and informative. The students were split into groups of thirty and they visited different workshops and presentations during the day. There was a tour of the college and I was glad to see the library for the first time. Sometimes students think that priests only read the Bible and so it was a fantastic opportunity for them to see the library and be told of the variety of books available. Many students did not realise the depth of the curriculum at a seminary.

Some Sisters of Charity from Kingstanding in Birmingham gave a talk and so did some Dominican friars from Oxford. I led a workshop with Sister Maria from Mater Ecclesiae Convent. We didn't tell the students anything about her and they had to question her and build up a profile and vocation timeline. There were some really good exploratory questions and some more superficial fact-finding. In the end we learned lots about Sister Maria's sense of vocation and that she likes chocolates and prefers cats to dogs.

The day ended with Mass in the college chapel. It was lovely the way that they blended the songs together and slowed down some of the songs that we sing too fast in school. I tend to speed everything up in school and favour fast and loud rather than quiet and reflective. It worked well today and made we wonder whether I should slow down the worship songs that we sing. There were a few issues with sitting in choir, as the students are not used to facing each other during Mass, but it was an absolutely wonderful day and we intend to repeat it again next year. The only real deficiency was the lack of reflection on lay vocations and this is something that I will need to develop. The Mass was offered for all those present, that they may know God's purpose in their lives.

Lately all of the readings set for Mass have wonderfully set the foundation for the day and our Mass readings today continued this pattern,

> Now when Jesus saw great crowds around him, he gave orders to go over to the other side. And a scribe came up and said to him, 'Teacher, I will follow you wherever you go.' And Jesus said to him, 'Foxes have holes, and birds of the air have nests; but the Son of man has nowhere to lay his head.' Another of the disciples said to him, 'Lord, let me first go and bury my father.' But Jesus said to him, 'Follow me, and leave the dead to bury their own dead.' (Matthew 8:18-22)

I couldn't have picked a better reading to underpin what we sought to share today.

The staff – *Wednesday 1st July*

Apart from Mass at lunchtime, I deliberately set the whole day apart to spend with staff members. In many schools people seem to be at a low ebb at the moment. It has been a long year and staff are weary. Education is a rapidly changing world and many teachers can feel weighed down by the demands that are placed on them. Those who have faith seem to cope better, but even for them there is little room for the spiritual, as they become focused on survival. Busier timetables, academisation, exam preparation and administration, compound what is already a hectic, pressurised and exhausting profession. I hear many people speak about teachers working short hours and having long holidays, but only those who have worked in education really know the burden that they carry. I worry for many staff at this time, and their well-being. Teaching is a vocation but teachers also have a vocation to be a parent, a son or daughter. All too often the life outside can be neglected.

So I drank lots of coffee, chatted in store cupboards, prayed in offices and most importantly listened.

The Swimming Gala – *Friday 3rd July*
(St Thomas the Apostle)

Today is the feast of St Thomas the Apostle and at Mass we heard the well-known account of Thomas' doubting:

> Now Thomas, one of the twelve, called the Twin, was not with them when Jesus came. So the other disciples told him, 'We have seen the Lord.' But he said to them, 'Unless I see in his hands the print of the nails, and place my finger in the mark of the nails, and place my hand in his side, I will not believe.' Eight days later, his disciples were again in the house, and Thomas was with them. The doors were shut,

but Jesus came and stood among them, and said, 'Peace be with you.' Then he said to Thomas, 'Put your finger here, and see my hands; and put out your hand, and place it in my side; do not be faithless, but believing.' Thomas answered him, 'My Lord and my God!' Jesus said to him, 'Have you believed because you have seen me? Blessed are those who have not seen and yet believe.' (John 20:24-29)

During the homily, we thought about what it means to have doubts and how doubts are a normal part of being people of faith. Despite his initial questioning, St Thomas went on to great things. I always feel sorry for St Thomas and feel that I would have probably acted in the same way as he did.

A small number of pupils in school belong to the Syro-Malabar community, which is an Indian form of Catholicism with roots in the south of India. They celebrate St Thomas as the one who took the faith to India. Today we gave thanks and prayed for the local Keralan community in Nuneaton.

After Mass a small group of staff and students walked the short distance to St Joseph's Primary School. Here we practised some of the songs that we will be using for the Year 6 confirmation next week. We have been asked to lead some of the music and have managed to get together a band for the night.

Towards the end of the morning I made my way to the most nerve-racking event in my annual calendar, the Swimming Gala. Different students compete for their houses as part of this annual competition. Every year, since I have worked at the school, I have taken part in the Staff vs Students Relay Race. For the last few weeks I have been swimming in the evenings just to ensure that I will not show myself up in front of my colleagues and students.

It is important to show willing and be part of the fun of the community but I am not sure how many years I will continue to take part in this particular event.

14th Week in Ordinary Time

Prayer books – *Monday 6th July*

Twenty-five new prayer books arrived in the post this morning. The students who helped me unpack them were like little children on Christmas day opening their presents. For several months now we have been saying Morning Prayer from sheets which I print each day from the internet. This started as an experiment, as the students who come to Adoration in the mornings were interested in what I was reading from the Breviary. Over a number of weeks, they asked questions about the prayers that I was saying and expressed a wish to try to say them with me. To start with, it was a complete mess and we mostly made each other laugh as we said things in the wrong way and mispronounced words. It took me back to when I was a curate in Coventry, when we were always tripping up over words and laughing when mistakes were made. But over the last few months the students and I have got into a pattern and I really enjoy having them to say the Office with me.

Now on most mornings at least fifteen of us gather in the presence of the Blessed Sacrament to recite the Office of Morning Prayer. We had a go at using the books for the first time today but the prayers flowed less well than the sheets because of all the different page changes that were needed. I felt like a bingo caller as I kept announcing the different page numbers. It will take a few more weeks to settle down but I will save time on all the printing. Having proper books makes the whole thing seem more official for the students in the same way that the new albs gave a new credibility to the altar servers. We were very grateful to Agnes, one of the volunteers from the local parish, who donated the cost of purchasing these new books.

Much of what we do in the chapel is fairly traditional. The most popular things that we have are the Mass, the rosary and Morning Prayer. I persevere with more informal worship and groups but these don't have the same impact or attendance. Celebrating the Mass, praying the rosary, exposing the Blessed Sacrament and reciting the Office are much easier to do than putting together more informal and creative liturgies and yet I have come to the realisation that these very traditional forms of Catholic worship are what pupils respond to best, if the numbers are an indication. Music is the only aspect of what we do which is more informal and contemporary.

End of an era – *Wednesday 8th July*

After the lunchtime Mass I came home to the parish of St Joseph, Monks Kirby, where I was to celebrate a very special Mass. Deidre Towers is retiring after fifty-four years of working in Catholic education. She trained at St Paul's Teacher Training College at Newbold Revel and then worked at St Marie's Primary School in Rugby. Mrs Towers spent many years as head teacher at St Joseph's School until it closed in the 1990s. Following this she moved to teach RE to the Catholic children in the Revel Church of England School. This school is unique in that it provides for the Catholic children in terms of worship, RE and catechesis. She has prepared generations of St Joseph's children for their First Communion and confirmation and as a stalwart of the parish she provides a valuable link with the school.

The Mass was very celebratory and after the last hymn the choir sang 'Bring Me Sunshine' popularised by Morecombe and Wise, which brought tears to many eyes.

Receive the Holy Spirit – *Thursday 9th July*

The band gathered early this evening at Our Lady of the Angels Church for the confirmation service. We had been asked to play at this service and had prepared some songs during the Mass as well as some solos during the actual confirmation. Our involvement was requested to help build links with this primary school as we are now united in an academy.

Catholic confirmations are usually large occasions and this year almost sixty children were being confirmed by the bishop and so the church was packed to the rafters with confirmandi, parents, grandparents and supporters.

We had a good mixture of musicians from the school and Sixth Form who formed the band, which included piano, flute, guitars and drums. Three members of staff kindly gave up their evening to support the event. We had gathered together a singing group of about twenty students to support the music. Three students all sang their solos and despite initial nervousness, due to the large congregation, they really did themselves proud. During all the solos, there was a tangible silence in the congregation. I think the people present appreciated the bravery and commitment of these young students. Apart from the drums being a little loud, the music was very well received and the bishop gave a warm thanks to the students at the end of the Mass, which has really boosted their confidence. I was really pleased with how the students played and was thankful for all the effort that had gone into practising over the last few weeks.

Castanets – *Friday 10th July*

During Mass today we had some lovely new music which the musicians played during Communion. However, I had a surprise when a student, who is not usually part of the music group, pulled out some castanets during the Gospel Acclamation and started playing them. He managed to keep up with the rhythm but it was a little bit of a surprise as I had not been warned beforehand. Apparently he had briefed the band but wanted to surprise me. It is good that students want to contribute and it does make things feel far more spontaneous although it would be nice to know first. They were a gift from his grandmother.

In today's Gospel reading we heard about the dangers that were to be faced by the disciples:

> Behold, I send you out as sheep in the midst of wolves; so be wise as serpents and innocent as doves. Beware of men; for they will deliver you up to councils, and flog you in their synagogues, and you will be dragged before governors and kings for my sake, to bear testimony before them and the Gentiles. When they deliver you up, do not be anxious how you are to speak or what you are to say; for what you are to say will be given to you in that hour; for it is not you who speak, but the Spirit of your Father speaking through you. Brother will deliver up brother to death, and the father his child, and children will rise against parents and have them put to death; and you will be hated by all for my name's sake. But he who endures to the end will be saved. When they persecute you in one town, flee to the next; for truly, I say to you, you will not have gone through all the towns of Israel, before the Son of man comes. (Matthew 10:16-23)

All ministry and Christian vocation can feel a little like this at times. Work with young people will often result in facing indifference and hostility. Schools bring us into contact with all sorts of people, many of whom do not understand the Gospel or the Catholic faith. Having a strong faith is therefore essential to see us through the more challenging days. Building a network of support is also necessary. School chaplaincy can be lonely without support. Lay and ordained chaplains should seek to build support and teams within schools but also networks outside of the immediate school environment. Meeting with other chaplains as well as a spiritual director is something that I believe is indispensable.

15th Week in Ordinary Time

Last Monday – *Monday 13th July*

Rose leaves at the end of this week after working as a supply teacher during this year. Whilst her time in school has been short, she has been a regular supporter of the chapel and has faithfully attended the Monday morning Mass. In thanksgiving and to say farewell I celebrated Mass for her intentions today.

As usual, we said Morning Prayer after Mass and are slowly getting used to using the lovely new prayer books. Students continue to tell me that they enjoy this time together and we share the leading of psalms and readings between us. It creates a good opportunity for students to start leading worship in what is a small, intimate and supportive group. After we had finished there were a few minutes before the bell was due to ring and so I explained the importance of saying these prayers. I shared how what we do is part of the Church's corporate prayer and the Office provides a link to our brothers and sisters throughout the world. The result of this is a recognition that we are not praying in isolation but in union with all of God's Church.

Praying the psalms, canticles and readings ensures that our gathering is rooted in God's word. We pray in the presence of the Blessed Sacrament in the monstrance on the altar and so are bathed in His presence and nourished by His word. Students may not understand the complexity of the psalms or the readings but we are building a pattern and reliance on prayer as the bedrock for the school day and ultimately, our lives.

The Office can be a struggle at times. It may often feel burdensome and heavy but when we pray as a group I really get the feeling that we are being soaked in prayer.

Noticeboards – *Wednesday 15th July*

Throughout my time in school chaplaincy I have grown in the realisation that this form of ministry very much is at the fore of Jesus' desire to bring the Good News to the poor. So much of a school chaplain's time is devoted to students who struggle in many ways. Often the students I meet with most are the ones who find fitting in hard and experience challenges relating to their peers. This is even the case, to some extent, with those who come to chapel and support the activities that I run. Today's Gospel reading made me think about this today,

> At that time Jesus declared, 'I thank you, Father, Lord of heaven and earth, that you have hidden these things from the wise and understanding and revealed them to infants; yes, Father, for such was your gracious will. All things have been delivered to me by my Father; and no one knows the Son except the Father, and no one knows the Father except the

Son and any one to whom the Son chooses to reveal him.' (Matthew 11:25-27)

The chaplaincy has several noticeboards around the school and today after much nagging I agreed that two students could take responsibility for one board each. I was a little apprehensive as they are an important source of communication. The keen pair had some good ideas and so I provided the materials and let them loose. I have agreed to leave the boards in place until the beginning of next term but if the displays are good I may leave them up for longer. Student participation is important but this sort of thing makes me realise that I only allow this participation to go so far. The quality of the noticeboards reflects on the chaplaincy and also on me and I must confess that I was worried that if the quality was poor, other staff may think it was my handiwork. I suppose that this is a form of vanity. I am glad that students are enthusiastic about taking responsibility and hope that I will be pleasantly surprised by the results.

This afternoon was spent with Sixth Form and main school students practising the music for the confirmation Mass which takes place tomorrow night.

One hundred and thirty years – *Thursday 16th July*

Tonight we said a very sad farewell to six staff who are retiring after a combined service of one hundred and thirty years. They have all been exceptional servants of the school and their achievement speaks a great deal about the vocation to be a teacher.

The evening began with Mass in the Sixth Form LRC. Each member of staff who is retiring had chosen a hymn which we sang during the Mass. Imelda, the special educational needs coordinator, had worked really hard to produce a beautiful Mass booklet which also contained a short biography of each of the retirees. During the homily I preached on the passage from Matthew 11 where Jesus promises to be a light burden to those who come to him for rest,

> Come to me, all who labour and are heavy laden, and I will give you rest. Take my yoke upon you, and learn from me; for I am gentle and lowly in heart, and you will find rest for your souls. For my yoke is easy, and my burden is light. (Matthew 11:28-30)

I reflected upon what a Christian model of retirement should be in relation to this passage. Jesus' burden will always be light but finding rest in him does not mean inactivity. To have a vocation as a teacher is an incredibly important ministry and this sense of vocation does not necessarily disappear upon retirement. It may take different forms but God still calls us on to new and different challenges. The people we celebrated tonight are those whose working lives have had a strong dimension of service to others and they are not the kind of people to just put their feet up. I am sure that they will find new and meaningful ways of employing their gifts, talents and abilities.

It was lovely to see many former staff and the families of the retirees present. It was an evening of mixed emotions. One member of staff presented a picture to be placed in the chapel, which I blessed during the Mass. She has been a stalwart of the chapel and has taught in the school since before I was born. I have regularly reminded her of this over the last few years. Many of those retiring will continue to be supply teachers and a couple will work on a part-time basis in an administrative capacity, but it is still very much the end of an era. The night ended with a wonderful party with speeches and presentations in the main school hall.

It is finished – *Friday 17th July*

There is a real sense of completion at the end of a school year. Over the last few weeks, things have been so busy and as I arrived at school this morning I knew the end was in sight. So much has been done during this year and so many relationships strengthened and developed. I feel exhausted but also satisfied with all that has happened. But the ending will be short-lived as in seven weeks' time it will all start again, this rapidly cycling school year.

After a really celebratory Mass this morning, I spent the day tying up loose ends. I always empty the tabernacle and consume the remaining hosts and for me this is always a symbolic and final act of the year. At Mass this morning I preached about Jesus being the master of the sabbath but also the master of the school year. This related to our Gospel reading,

> At that time Jesus went through the grain fields on the sabbath; his disciples were hungry, and they began to pluck ears of grain and to eat. But when the Pharisees saw it, they said to him, 'Look, your disciples are doing what is not lawful to do on the sabbath.' He said to them, 'Have you not read what David did, when he was hungry, and those who were with him: how he entered the house of God and ate the bread of the Presence, which it was not lawful for him to eat nor for those who were with him, but only for the priests? Or have you not read in the law how on the sabbath the priests in the temple profane the sabbath, and are guiltless? I tell you, something greater than the temple is here. And if you had known what this means, "I desire mercy, and not sacrifice," you would not have condemned the guiltless. For the Son of man is lord of the sabbath.' (Matthew 12:1-8)

At break time I met with the Chaplaincy Council, servers and musicians for hot drinks and doughnuts. Everyone is so excited about the holidays but this is coupled with a certain weariness.

The working day ended at lunchtime with a final assembly, during which I led some prayers and gave a blessing. The pupils were released into the sunlight and the staff retreated to the hall where there were speeches from more staff that are leaving. A proportion of staff always moves on at the end of each year and careers will progress but it is always sad to say goodbye. School really is a fluid and dynamic community and in that sense being a chaplain to a school is like no other form of ministry. This keeps things fresh but always creates many challenges. For now, I am going to rest and enjoy the summer. September will come soon enough.

CHAPTER SEVEN

Taking stock of challenging issues faced by Catholics in secondary schooling in the UK

Chaplaincy does have something special and completely different to offer alongside other forms of help that are available to students in school. We should not be afraid to make this distinctive support available. This is also true of the whole Catholic school where a contrasting perspective can be provided alongside many therapies and interventions which are increasingly secular in their value bases.

There are multiple areas that chaplaincy can become involved and make a difference but here I provide just a few examples of particular areas where chaplaincy engagement can be significant and helpful.

Self-harm

Self-harm can affect anyone and there is no such thing as a typical self-harmer. It is not always an indicator of a mental illness and it can be something that emerges in people of any age, gender, social background or race. There are occasions when those who self-harm do not even realise that they are doing it, which is known as disassociation.

Since working with young people, I have supported a wide range of individuals who self-harm in some way. This has always been in tandem with other professionals. Often it is something that will not last for long but for others it can be something longer-term that becomes seriously damaging.

Students can self-harm to bring control over situations that they find themselves in. They may do it because they feel isolated and have low self-esteem. Harming their body can be as a result of frustration, despair, anger, shame, depression, resentment, loss and isolation. There are multiple reasons and explanations. The majority of students who have these feelings do not resort to self-harm, but for some their experiences become so unbearable that hurting themselves becomes a way of dealing with what they face.

Self-harm will often provide a sense of control that may be missing in other aspects of the student's life experience. The person may view self-harm as a form of self-punishment which is linked to a heavy sense of guilt.

Students have often told me that hurting themselves can become a release, making them feel alive. I once worked with one young person who saw that letting blood allowed bad feelings to drain away from her. Often it is also a cry for help and a way to communicate how bad things have become when words become difficult to find.

One challenge is the often addictive nature of self-harm and breaking a habit can be extremely hard. Such complexity means that the need to involve others with expertise is paramount.

Secular external agencies, such as counselling services, will often have never worked with chaplains and may not understand what underpins a chaplain's work. At times some professionals may have preconceptions about faith-based support and their own prejudices will need to be gently challenged. It is therefore essential that a chaplain is able to articulate about their role, responsibilities and the framework within which they minister. It is also vitally important that chaplains function within their own level competency and don't become involved in work outside their knowledge and expertise, as the credibility of chaplaincy is at stake.

Self-harm: What can chaplaincy offer?

> The Lord is near to the broken-hearted,
> and saves the crushed in spirit.
> Many are the afflictions of the righteous;
> but the Lord delivers him out of them all.
> (Psalm 34:8-19, *ESVUK*)

Self-harm is something that should be talked about. If it is a cry for help to see if anyone cares, then chaplaincy has a valuable role in showing compassion and interest in the young person's situation. A chaplain can open up much wider possibilities and can place suffering and anxiety into a wider cosmic context. Our role is to offer a listening ear and advice, but also to bring an awareness of God's presence within the situation of suffering. We can emphasise that God cares, that he is at the heart of all that is going on, and that he calls the young person into transformation. Those we work with are a new creation in Christ, the old self has passed away and a new reality exists:

> Therefore, if any one is in Christ, he is a new creation;
> the old has passed away, behold, the new has come. All
> this is from God, who through Christ reconciled us

to himself and gave us the ministry of reconciliation.
(2 Corinthians 5:17-18, *RSVCE*)

We can journey with young people to help them see that their relationship with Jesus results in a new creation. The old may creep back in but it has been put to death with the death of Christ. Enabling others to be transformed is therefore a marvellous part of a chaplain's work because it is rooted in the cross of Christ. Working with resistant and doubting teenagers to see this is the more challenging part.

Where the cause of self-harm is low self-esteem, chaplaincy can also have a great deal to share in relation to the intrinsic dignity of the human person. This is expressed well in one of the four constitutions resulting from the Second Vatican Council: 'The root reason for human dignity lies in man's call to communion with God. From the very circumstance of his origin man is already invited to converse with God' (*Gaudium et Spes*, 19).

All people are created in the image of God (Genesis 1:27) and this is where our dignity is rooted. For those with a sense of low self-worth, investigating this relationship can be invaluable. However, growing in the understanding of our relationship with God brings responsibilities. St Paul calls us to glorify God in our bodies (Romans 6:12-14). If we are truly made in God's image, then damaging our bodies or neglecting our health can be seen as devaluing this image. St Paul again warns of the consequences of neglecting or abusing the gift of our bodies: 'Do you not know that your body is a temple of the Holy Spirit within you, which you have from God? You are not your own; you were bought with a price. So glorify God in your body' (1 Corinthians 6:19-20).

The idea that we are not our own and are custodians of the body, is something worth exploring. I have led many group sessions of young people with low self-esteem, and considering biblical ideas about the body is something that students have seemed to engage well with. The privilege and responsibility of a relationship with our creator is rooted in the teaching of the Catholic Church:

> Life and physical health are precious gifts entrusted to us by God. We must take reasonable care of them, taking into account the needs of others and the common good. (*Catechism of the Catholic Church*, 2288)

I have always been greatly impressed by the Twelve Step Model that was developed by Alcoholics Anonymous to help people overcome addiction and damaging behaviours. The approach has been used by other groups over time and because of its emphasis on a 'greater being' it is a useful model for school chaplains to be aware of. I have adopted many of its insights in relation to both group work in school and one-to-one support with students. The twelve steps are not appropriate to use out of context but I always appreciate the way that they emphasise growing realisation of problems with an understanding of our relationship with God. The original twelve steps are as follows:

1. We admit we were powerless over addiction – that our personal situation had become unmanageable.
2. To believe that a Power greater than ourselves could restore us to sanity.
3. Made a decision to turn our will and our lives over to the care of God as we understood God.
4. Made a searching and fearless moral inventory of ourselves.
5. Admitted to God, to ourselves and to another human being the exact nature of our wrongs.
6. Were entirely ready to have God remove all these defects of character.

7. Humbly asked God to remove our shortcomings.
8. Made a list of all persons we had harmed, and became willing to make amends to them all.
9. Made direct amends to such people wherever possible, except when to do so would injure them or others.
10. Continued to take personal inventory and when we were wrong promptly admitted it.
11. Sought through prayer and meditation to improve our conscious contact with God as we understood God, praying only for knowledge of God's will for us and the power to carry that out.
12. Having had a spiritual awakening as the result of these steps, we tried to carry this message to other addicts, and to practise these principles in all our affairs.

In a busy school, chaplaincy can offer space and time for pupils to explore their feelings and anxieties. Creating safe space to explore is something which I have always sought to do. It is here where a ministry of availability comes into its own. Often there will be waiting lists for other forms of help and in some cases several weeks can lapse before other agencies become involved. Chaplaincy can react quickly to situations as we are on the ground, know the territory, understand some of the relationships and most importantly are known to the young person already.

Sexualisation

One of the great issues and challenges facing many young people today is increasing sexualisation. The ubiquitous and hugely problematic culture of pornography cannot and should not be underestimated. Many young people face the temptations of peer pressure and their own curiosity to access online pornography. This may result in behaviour developing which can be addictive and ultimately destructive.

Those working with young people today need to be aware of the risks and be informed about this negative culture that so many today are immersed in. Chaplaincy, teachers and youth workers can often be on the front line and we are regularly the first adults that young people will turn to. It is important that we are ready and prepared so that our response is safe, appropriate and supportive.

Our response also needs to be part of our proclamation of the Good News of Jesus. Safeguarding the vulnerable, setting high standards and showing a new and better way are all Gospel principles that should be woven into this aspect of our work and intervention.

Developing awareness and self-protection

There have been a number of occasions where I have worked with a young person who has encountered online pornography by accident, often through pop-ups of misleading web links. They have often been upset by this and feel a sense of shame. In many instances students will seek the support of a chaplain because they don't know what to do and need advice. Those who are most affected by this are often young people who have not been supported by parents or other adults to be prepared and to be safe. This can often be a shock which deeply impacts upon the young person and takes away some of their innocence.

It is important if children and young people are using the internet that they know how to stay safe and also that they have a strategy about what to do if they are concerned about something that they have seen, experienced or heard others talk about. Parents may perceive that they are protecting their children by not discussing such issues or sometimes feel embarrassed to talk about delicate topics, but if these matters are not addressed then our children's well-being could be adversely affected. Our vocation as parents to prepare our children is a little like the way Jesus sends his disciples into the world,

> Behold, I send you out as sheep in the midst of wolves; so be wise as serpents and innocent as doves (Matthew 10:16).

Making children aware of dangers helps them to be wise in their choices and does not necessarily mean that we take away their innocence or coarsen them. Rather we can actually protect and safeguard their innocence by equipping them for the world.

Sometimes young people access pornography via the internet because they are curious and have questions about sex and relationships. They can be seeking answers to questions that they feel unable to ask parents or adults that they trust. If we do not speak naturally to our children about issues of sex, sexuality and relationships then we take the risk that our children will turn to the internet. Inadvertently we can make the porn industry educators in our child's development.

There are many websites providing advice to young people, parents, and those who work with children, about awareness of pornography and issues of sex education generally. These can be very helpful, although as Catholics we do need to be careful. Websites and resources which are developed by trusted organisations may not always be consistent with the teaching of the Catholic Church on issues of human sexuality.

Use of pornography and body image

There is a pretty general consensus that where young people are exposed to sexually explicit images and material they are at a much greater risk of developing unrealistic body images. Individuals who work with young people will regularly encounter those who have low self-esteem which is often linked to issues of how they perceive that they look.

One of the challenges of working with young people is to help them understand that images they see in magazines, on the television and on the internet are often not real. The cult of celebrity is also partly to blame for this rising crisis. We risk having a generation of young people whose perception of the body is completely distorted from that which is reasonable and normal. I find it important to continue to share with young people that such images are false and often unhealthy.

If we are honest many of us have some issues with the way that we look. As we are reminded by the psalmist:

> I praise you, for I am fearfully and wonderfully made.
> Wonderful are your works; that I know very well.
> (Psalm 139:14).

Helping all people to gain a real and meaningful understanding that God made us the way we are is crucial in overcoming the negative pressure to conform to unrealistic stereotypes. What is inside is what really counts in God's eyes. To God it is the only thing that is important. Communicating this particular nugget of good news has to be part of a chaplain's proclamation.

Peer pressure

There are times when young people feel a great pressure to watch pornography online. Sadly, many young people are not ashamed of watching explicit material and will talk about it openly amongst their friends and peers. This places a significant pressure on other young people who desire to conform and fit in with those around them. We see a growing situation amongst young people where watching pornography becomes normalised and part of the culture of friendship groups and young people's social networks.

It is important that young people know that not everyone watches pornography and that it is certainly not a normal thing to do. Our response should be appropriate to the young person's age. As a parent it is tempting to merely tell a child that something is wrong without giving deeper reasons. We have to be prepared and equipped to say why pornography is wrong and help a young person explore why it is not in their best interests and inappropriate.

Sexting

A recent phenomenon amongst young people is what has become known as 'sexting'. This involves sharing explicit images through mobile phones, email or online. Often including images that young people have found on the internet, this can, more worryingly, also feature explicit images of themselves or their friends.

For all involved with young people, it is important to understand the risks so that we can support those we work with to keep safe. It is worrying that a number of young people see this as a normal thing to do. Sometimes high profile celebrities have admitted to sexting and so this gives it a sense of normality which needs to be challenged and addressed. This presence of sexting can be underestimated and is far more common than one might expect. Awareness is essential.

Many young people do not realise the lasting effect that sexting can have upon their lives. Once images are shared there is always the risk that someone has saved or shared them. It is important that young people are made aware that what they share becomes public and may in the future resurface and possibly be used against them. Prevention and education is therefore the best approach in protecting and safeguarding the dignity and life chances of children.

If images are shared more widely it can lead to the young person being stigmatised by their peers and bullied. I am aware of a situation where a child was blackmailed by someone who had received images of them. The emotional impact also should not be underestimated and can contribute to mental ill health, anxiety and even in extreme cases suicidal thoughts and ideas.

It is important that we speak to young people about the risks. Parents who buy mobile phones, tablets and computers for their children have a huge responsibility to ensure that they use these devices safely and appropriately.

A Catholic school has a prophetic message to share with children about propriety, sexual acts outside of marriage and the need to have self-respect. Whilst this may seem at odds with the value of the world we should be fearless in our positive proclamation of the Church's teaching. The mental physical and sexual well-being of our children is at stake.

It is also vitally important that we know what to do if the children or the young people we work with have been involved in sexting. For those who work in schools this will require us following our safeguarding procedures and involving those staff appointed to lead on safeguarding issues. In such situations we cannot guarantee confidentiality.

There is a need to act quickly before images are shared more widely. Involving the police may be necessary, particularly in situations where a young person reports that they have been pressured or forced to share images. Childline is a useful resource and they can work with the Internet Watch Foundation to try and have the image removed.

There is the possibility of setting up parental controls on your child's phone. Often this is not popular with young people and will not always be foolproof but it remains a positive action that we can do.

The place of the Faith

Our best remedy against the culture of sexualisation and pornography is to help our children to develop a living faith. In today's culture there can be some resistance to sharing our faith and evangelising our children. I routinely hear parents say that they wish to let their children choose for themselves what they believe regarding religious faith. However, we do not apply this to other aspects of life and so why neglect the Faith? There are risks with not handing on an active faith.

Bringing our children up to personally know Jesus can equip them to live in the world with all its temptations and dilemmas. Children not grounded in Christ can be vulnerable to the world and thus unable to spiritually mature into adults who make moral decisions based on sound faith. Jesus made it abundantly clear that He wants us to educate children about Him and inspire them to trust in Him,

> And they were bringing children to him, that he might touch them; and the disciples rebuked them. But when Jesus saw it he was indignant, and said to them, 'Let the children come to me, do not hinder them; for to such belongs the kingdom of God. Truly, I say to you, whoever does not receive the kingdom of God like a child shall not enter it.' And he took them in his arms and blessed them, laying his hands upon them. (Mark 10:13-16)

The Catholic school has an important place in ensuring that this relationship is fostered and developed. This is why we need more staff in our schools who are prepared to live as disciples of Jesus, leading others in the way of truth. Passing on this living faith is not only about verbally communicating truths, but also modelling it in our lifestyles and positive relationships. Neglecting this places our children at risk. If children learn to accept and explore the values, moral teaching and wisdom of Jesus then hopefully they will live by them and be kept safe.

The sexualisation of our young people is now deeply culturally imbedded within many young people's lives. Challenging the prevailing norms and presenting something better is the only way of formulating a longer-term solution. At the heart of Evangelisation is the transforming of cultures and the changing of lives with the Good News of Jesus. Without transformation we are only firefighting the problem and it will no doubt get worse as things develop with successive generations.

I find it very sad that so many young people that I work with do not have a living faith. Catholicism is often cultural (and barely even that sometimes) and the moral and social teaching of the Church is alien. We have inoculated many of our children with a lukewarm version of the faith which leaves them with little in the way of a moral compass to direct them through life. They also do not understand the great hope that Jesus presents to us.

I affirm that any preventative safeguarding to protect our children begins with Evangelisation and the knowledge of a loving Saviour. This is why faithful and faith-filled Catholic schools are urgently needed in our society.

Presenting healthy relationships

Sadly, today many young people experience first-hand relationships which are dysfunctional or broken. When I was at school the majority of my fellow pupils still lived with both parents and the main image that we had of a family was of siblings living with both parents. There were some parents who had separated but this was far more unusual. Today's children are presented with increasingly complex family compositions, not all of which are of course dysfunctional. We cannot assume that being a teenager is the same experience as when we were young. The context and the culture is massively different and rapidly changing.

It is important for young people to understand that the relationships they see in pornography are very different from a normal healthy one. Pornography presents a sexual relationship without responsibility. Over time if a young person is exposed to pornography they can easily gain a view that casual sex is normal and worthwhile. This view is often reinforced in popular culture and the media and so a young Catholic who may wish to live according to their faith may face a great deal of confusion and conflict.

The challenge today is presenting an image of a positive relationship when so many marriages and families are divided in some way. As Catholics we cannot afford to shy away from teaching about the importance of marriage. Presenting positive and responsible role models and ideals is vitally important to the well-being of young people. Catholic education, chaplaincy, parish youth workers and faithful families can offer so much positivity in guiding young people in making sense of sex and relationships. In situations where there has been divorce and separation it is important that young people have the opportunity to discuss and reflect. Parents should be as honest with their children as possible.

Issues of human sexuality faced in school chaplaincy

As chaplains we have the privileged position to help children to develop through their formative years. This means that chaplains and all who work in Catholic education are in a great position of trust.

Issues of human sexuality will present themselves regularly on a personal level, as students will seek guidance and support to deal with all manner of feelings, urges and life experiences relating to sex and sexuality. In this area the main focus of a chaplain or anyone else should be to develop a culture of pastoral sensitivity, love and care. Students will have often sought advice because a chaplain, teacher or other school worker is viewed as someone who is trusted and readily available. It is important that this trusted relationship is maintained in order to continue to offer the young person a safe place within which to explore the issues that they face.

Whilst a school's response to individuals should always be compassionate, there is also the centrally important need to teach and share what the Church and Jesus has to say on matters of human sexuality and relationships. In my experience this has always been done in a healthy, respectful and balanced way. Those outside the Catholic system may have their own prejudices and misconceptions about how sex education and relationships are presented in Catholic schools. I have never witnessed issues of human sexuality being discussed in ways which would undermine or diminish anyone personally. It is this freedom of Catholic schools to teach about sex and relationships, in an open, positive and honest way founded upon a Catholic moral and philosophical foundation, which is often at risk today in an increasingly secular world.

Wider society's values and views relating to sexuality and LGBT issues have changed dramatically over the last twenty-five years and those who work in chaplaincy and Catholic schools need to be aware of the challenges that this new reality brings. Catholic schools should be places where truths about human sexuality can be upheld whilst at the same time being safe places for young people to explore their thoughts, feelings and emotions.

Western society has largely separated love from sex. The media has had a major role in downgrading the values of stability, fidelity and family life which was once taken for granted by most in Britain. This has shaped and fashioned many young people's perspectives when it comes to thinking about relationships, marriage and authentic human love. Casual sex without responsibility is often seen as the norm in a world which seems to be increasingly morally ambiguous. Added to this, an increasing number of parents will be separated or divorced and so many young people do not have personal experience of marital stability. In this context all relationships, however fleeting or transient, can become viewed as having equal validity in many young people's thinking. Matters are complicated further because many young people are already sexually active or know peers who are. Sex has become something casual and trivial.

It is in this context that chaplaincy can bring a message of hope and stability. Re-establishing a proper sense of sexual expression can only begin to happen when human love and sexuality are once again seen as interdependent. The need for sex to be placed within the context of a lifelong relationship related to procreation is something that we should be able to communicate naturally and not defensively. Having the confidence to celebrate *marriage* as an expression of God's divine love is something that could be developed more coherently within many schools. This may be part of the RE curriculum but the celebration of marriage, like any other Christian vocation, should not just be the preserve of the RE department. Pastoral staff, heads of year and chaplains all have an important role in the sharing of the values of stability that marriage and family life can bring. Such staff will be all too aware of families where there is division and so this should also inform the approach that they take.

A pastoral sense of compassion for students struggling with issues of sexual orientation must be balanced with a very clear message that chastity is good, worthwhile and truly positive, a true freedom (and this is a message that should apply to all the young people we work with). With this in mind, alongside marriage, it is also imperative to present the value of celibacy and virginity. As St John Paul II states:

> Christian revelation recognizes two specific ways of realizing the vocation of the human person in its entirety, to love: marriage and virginity or celibacy. Either one is, in its own proper form, an actuation of the most profound truth of man, of his being 'created in the image of God.' Consequently, sexuality, by means of which man and woman give themselves to one another through the acts which are proper and exclusive to spouses, is by no means something purely biological, but concerns the innermost being of the human person as such. It is realized in a truly human way only if it is an integral part of the love by which a man and a woman commit themselves totally to one another until death. (*Familiaris Consortio*, 11)

This message does not attack others but provides an approach which is rooted in the love and goodness of God. We don't have to be negative when we have such a positive story to tell.

Part of the problem for schools is that the wider Church does not give a clear enough message about the value of marriage, celibacy and family life. Many ordinary Catholics are unclear themselves about what Church teaching is on issues of human sexuality. Homilies are rarely preached about such important issues. This is therefore something that needs developing in the wider Church and not just our schools. Often, Catholic schools can be made a scapegoat within the Catholic community when our young people leave the faith and do not know basic Church teaching. Bishops, clergy and parishes also need to be more proactive in leading our communities and guiding faithful Catholic families in the role as primary educators and nurturers of their children. Schools are at the coalface in this respect but they should not be left alone. A school can only be strong if it has steadfast bishops behind them.

Conclusion

There is no ministry like school chaplaincy. It offers a wonderful opportunity to share the faith with young people during their most formative years. I certainly have felt privileged to be able to walk alongside staff and students within the schools that I know.

I am a passionate advocate of Catholic education and our system of schools and colleges. I am also aware of the weaknesses within our schools and the storms of secularism which seek to undermine and undo the generations of hard toil that have established our work with children and young people. I am acutely aware that, 'If a kingdom is divided against itself, that kingdom cannot stand' (Mark 3:24). If we are to stand firm when there are those who seek to deconstruct Catholic education, then we must be steadfast as a Church and have high expectations of our schools and those who work in them. We cannot afford to let our schools be Catholic in name only. I believe that Catholics have not been assertive enough in this regard. Bishops, dioceses, priests, school governors, school leaders and teachers all need to play their role in calling to account our schools and supporting them to work out what it means to be a Catholic school in the 21st century in a post-Christian society.

We need to emulate the pioneers of Catholic education and take risks, make sacrifices, and most importantly be brave and not be apologetic about our Catholicism and the uniqueness of Jesus, his teaching and his sacraments.

Creating and sustaining a Culture of Vocation

Last week I attended celebrations for two teachers who were retiring after many decades of loyal and dedicated service within our Catholic schools. Between them they had clocked up over eighty years of commitment to nurturing our children. During the latter part of their careers they had even taught the grandchildren of some of those that they encountered when newly qualified. They had clearly touched the lives of many through their outstanding service and it made me realise why I still believe that Catholic schools are vital in the transformative work of the Gospel.

During the speeches it was heartening to hear that both were extremely grateful for their Catholic teacher training and perceived this to be foundational in the formation of their strong sense of vocation and longevity. Since being involved in Catholic schools I have encountered many fantastic people who trained as Catholic teachers with the intention of being in it for the long haul. I now recognise the presence of such devoted individuals as one of the hallmarks of a healthy and vibrant Catholic school.

As well as giving thanks for their personal dedication, I reflected privately that I was also sadly witnessing the passing of something much more. These were committed Catholics who had given their entire working lives to a vision of Catholic education.

Sadly, this seems to be a form of commitment that is slowly ebbing away. During last week's celebration, as I looked around the church and the function afterwards, I began to wonder where the next generation of this type of person was. Yes, there were fine and outstanding teachers who are committed to their work, but the pressures of modern education and all the expectations and demands placed upon staff mean that it is increasingly harder and unusual to remain in teaching for a whole career. I meet many teachers in the course of my week who are considering longer-term options outside of the profession.

A future challenge will be ensuring that younger staff members continue to develop that purposeful understanding of what it means to be a Catholic teacher in a Catholic school. This sense of vocation will only emerge when future teachers are animated by their own living faith. Catholic education will not thrive if those involved in it have a vague understanding of the Catholic faith and hold liberal views which are at odds with the moral teachings of the Church. A renewed culture rooted in faith and underpinned by first-class catechesis should be our aim.

I believe that we have a crisis of vocation in our schools which is far larger than the crisis of vocations to the priesthood. The situation is not without hope, but I am convinced that something of the pioneering spirit which founded our schools will have to be rediscovered in order to find a solution. Complacency is an option but it will ultimately lead to the loss of a system of schools which was hard won.

After the restoration of the Catholic hierarchy in England and Wales, the bishops saw the great need for the education of the poor. Provision of schools and training of teachers was thought to be so important that it often came before the construction of church buildings. The Church had the vision and commitment to ensure that teachers were formed both in the faith and educational practice. Whilst there are still centres of excellence in terms of Catholic teacher training today, there are not enough to ensure that our schools have the quantity and calibre of teachers that we need. How can we recapture the missional charism of teaching that seems to have been lost over the last few decades?

Our Catholic schools present us with a great opportunity and give an amazing platform for engagement with the world which prevents the Church existing in a vacuum. Catholic schools were founded through great personal commitment and sacrificial giving at parish level as well as amongst the bishops. The whole Catholic community have a responsibility to support our schools. When was the last time you prayed for vocations to our schools or encouraged someone you know to think about the possibility of teaching as a life choice? Every faithful Catholic needs to become part of the solution.

To save Catholic education, do we need to give up some of our Catholic schools?

Rationalisation of parishes and masses in the face of reducing clergy numbers is certainly going to be a reality within the next few years. As the number of parishes and masses are reduced, do we also need to think about how we will continue to maintain other institutions including our Catholic schools?

Catholic schools currently make up one in ten of all school provision in England and Wales, with nearly 850,000 pupils educated in 2,245 schools. This is an incredible achievement, especially when considered that a higher proportion of Catholic schools are in deprived areas and that Catholic schools are often more diverse than average (34.5 per cent of pupils in our maintained primary schools are from ethnic minority backgrounds compared with a national figure of 28.5 per cent).

A vocations crisis

A significant challenge today is the recruitment and retention of Catholic staff. There remains a requirement that head teachers, deputy head teachers and those staff responsible for RE and Catholic life are practising Catholics. This is essential if the Catholic identity of a school is to be maintained and to grow. Here lies the problem. The number of applicants to such posts is falling. Recently, in a school that I know well, there was only one applicant for a head teacher vacancy, and this is not an isolated situation. The school in question was a good and attractive example, and a great deal of effort and imagination was put into the recruitment process. If we cannot recruit Catholic leaders for our schools, then what meaningful future is there?

To support the Catholic ethos of our schools and to ensure that we have leaders for the future we need many other staff, in addition to senior leaders, who can further the mission of our schools. While there are teachers and support staff who are non-Catholic who do a wonderful job in supporting the work of Catholic schools, there is no substitute for a fired-up Catholic who has a strong sense of vocation.

In 2013, in English Catholic schools 69 per cent of primary teachers and 44.2 per cent of secondary school teachers were Catholic, but this number is thought to be reducing year-on-year as long-serving staff retire.

Yet when was the last time that you heard a homily in which teaching as a vocation was promoted? When did your parish last have a day of Adoration praying for vocations to our schools? We have a crisis in vocations, not just to the priesthood but also to Catholic education.

This will only change when we build a culture which celebrates vocation amongst Catholics, staff who work in our schools, and those who may be considering a career in teaching.

We need to stop celebrating sympathy

One thing that I regularly hear in schools is that certain members of staff are praised for being 'sympathetic' to the Catholic ethos. If Catholic schools are to be missional, is sympathy enough? It was determination, commitment, hard work and sacrifice that founded our schools. No mission will bear fruit if those who are supposed to be advancing it are passively sympathetic. We need people who are driving forward the vision with passion, enthusiasm, imagination and, most importantly, Faith.

Worse still are lapsed Catholics who staff our schools. Only attending Mass when you are paid is certainly not an example of discipleship and faithfulness. Yet I meet so many people who are 'school Catholics'. These people say they support the ethos and receive the sacraments at school masses but are strangers to their local parish on a Sunday. Why would you trust someone with helping to hand on the faith to your children when they don't live the faith in their own lives? School chaplaincy has a wonderful role in offering support and catechesis to such people to enable them to walk with Jesus. This is very much about evangelising those Catholics whose faith has grown cold.

We have to be careful here, as many of our schools could not function without non-Catholic staff. For generations we have failed to raise up enough teachers from our parishes. In many schools I know, there are wonderful non-Catholic staff who are committed and bring values from their own faith to bear within their own sense of vocation. This does not change the great need for more Catholic staff in the mission of our schools.

Governing our Catholic schools

The trustees of our Catholic schools (often the local dioceses or religious orders who founded the school) have the legal right to appoint foundation governors. Appointing foundation governors, who form the majority of the governing body, helps to ensure that the school is operating according to the teaching of the Church and has a Catholic ethos. Such governors are therefore essential in supporting and maintaining the mission of schools.

The difficulty here lies in finding people willing to undertake the role. It is also imperative that we have the right candidates with the necessary skills and abilities. School governance is now more complicated than it has ever been. With the ongoing introduction of academies, OFSTED, statutory requirements, Section 48 inspections and a whole plethora of other developments, the demands on governors are substantial. I know from my own experience as a chair of governors that many hours are now taken up with meetings and fulfilling all my other duties and the expectations placed upon me.

As our parishes get smaller and fewer, parishioners are older and more stretched. Many governing bodies and academy boards of directors carry vacancies. In my own parish I have to rack my brain and make appeals every time a vacancy arises. It is a problem that will only increase.

Catholic numbers

The aim of the Church is to provide a school place for every Catholic child. In some areas the Church is struggling to meet the demand for places, while in others schools are struggling to recruit pupils and Catholic numbers are falling.

The loss in many areas of free school transport is a major factor in the reduction of baptised Catholics on school rolls. Parents, especially in poorer areas, cannot find the necessary finance to fund their child's transport. One local authority area charges families £630 a child each year. This is prohibitive for many working-class families (especially for those who have read *Humanae Vitae*!). Many parents have no choice but to select a non-Catholic school for their children.

Sacramental provision

With the reduction in clergy numbers there is a real pressure to maintain sacramental provision in schools. When a parish closes, the school will often remain. There are many examples where the parish school is still functioning following the closure or amalgamation of parishes. This can often leave priests with multiple schools in their parishes and comes with competing demands and expectations.

Many schools don't even have a weekly Mass now and this is only likely to get worse. Children who don't worship in their local parishes also don't have much exposure to the Mass and other liturgies in their school. We risk leaving children with a vague and superficial experience of genuine Catholic worship.

The sacraments and worship should be the backbone of a Catholic school. These are gifts that make us distinct in Christ and have the power to heal and transfigure whole communities in education. At a time when sacraments are most needed, schools and families are often becoming less sacramental. Clergy are overworked but that does not remove the fact that schools are one of our biggest areas of mission and we neglect tilling the soils of our schools at our peril.

The introduction of lay chaplains in some schools has been one answer, but this is no substitute for priestly ministry. Lay chaplains have a valuable and much needed role but often postholders experience poor pay and have an uncertain role and status in some schools. Formation and training is also an area that needs developing for lay chaplains to fully flourish. For a lay chaplain to properly flourish they need to work in partnership with strong priestly ministry.

Rationalisation?

We hear lots about the rationalisation of parishes because of falling numbers of vocations and parishioners. When was the last time that we heard about the rationalisation of our schools? We could be in a situation where parishes and masses get fewer but schools increase. How will we sustain this if the main body of the Church is shrinking? Do our schools need to shrink to fit?

I write this as the government have lifted the bar on the number of Catholic pupils who can be admitted to new Catholic schools that are founded. Part of me celebrates this move as it will allow for the increase in areas where more provision is needed. I also worry that we will continue to spread our resources more thinly. Catholic schools do an excellent job precisely because of the Catholic educational philosophy and ethos which underpins them, but without Catholic faithful amongst the staff and a sacramental underpinning we are creating something which cannot be sustained. The danger is, without change, our schools could become Catholic in name only.

Working within Catholic schools has brought me great blessings and the opportunity to minister to young people is a wonderful gift. They bring freshness, inquisitiveness and an honesty which priests rarely encounter in other contexts.

This book has aimed to highlight the ups and downs, joys and frustrations of working in schools. It is my hope and prayer that more Catholics will step up to the challenge and serve our school communities. Faith-filled people can make a great difference and we need them more than ever.